THE LAW

ON

ECONOMIC CRIMES
IN ZAMBIA

A Concise Guide

JOSEPH CHIRWA

GIFT *Certificate*

TO:

_____

_____

FROM:

_____

_____

DATE: _____

Would you like to buy a copy of
THE LAW ON ECONOMIC CRIMES IN ZAMBIA?

PLEASE VISIT:
http://www.diamondbooks.ca

THE LAW
ON
ECONOMIC CRIMES
IN ZAMBIA

A Concise Guide

Joseph Chirwa

He is an academic and law researcher based in the City and Province
of Lusaka in the Republic of Zambia..

DIAMOND™
BOOKS

www.diamondbooks.ca

TORONTO, CANADA – 2022

UNITED STATES, CANADA, UNITED KINGDOM, INDIA, ZAMBIA

THE LAW ON ECONOMIC CRIMES IN ZAMBIA

DIAMOND ™
BOOKS
www.diamondbooks.ca

PUBLISHED IN CANADA

Published in Canada by DIAMOND BOOKS ™, an imprint
of
DIAMOND PUBLISHERS CANADA
http://www.diamondpublishers.com

DIAMOND BOOKS ™ - REGISTERED TRADEMARK IN CANADA AND WORLDWIDE.

FIRST EDITION: OCTOBER, 2022

PAPERBACK EDITION : ISBN: 978-1-77375-274-7

PRINTED IN CANADA

FOREWORD

The backbone of any stable country is its economy and most specially its economic stability. This is very reason why institutions have been put in place to protect the economy. Zambia is no exception to this state of affairs as like many countries it is a victim of economic crimes. The handbook on economic crimes is an attempt to give a glimpse on the law surrounding this field of law. The book traverses both the legal and institutional framework in the area of corruption, money laundering, economic sabotage and terrorism among others. It addresses the functions of institutions such as the Anti-Corruption Commission, Drug Enforcement Commission, Anti-Money Laundering Unit and Zambia Revenue Authority among others.

This is a succinct yet comprehensive guide on economic crimes in Zambia. It is the hope of the author that this will spark interest in this particular field of law among authors, lawyers and practitioners in related fields.

Joseph Chirwa, Esq.

Advocate (Barrister and Solicitor) of the Superior Courts of Zambia,

Lusaka, 2022.

ABOUT THE AUTHOR

Joseph Chirwa is a practising lawyer with interest in criminal law, criminology and criminal justice, labour and employment relations as well immigration and refugee law. He is author of leading legal texts in Zambia which include among others the following: Chirwa on Tort- A Student Companion; Essential Text on Local Government Law in Zambia; A Concise Manual of Immigration, Refugee and Citizenship Law in Zambia; Commentary on Public Law in Zambia-Law, Politics and Governance; Medical Law and Ethics in Zambia; Criminal Procedure and Practice in Zambia – An Introduction; Understanding Professional Conduct and Ethics for Legal Practitioners in Zambia; Essential Text on Medical Negligence in Zambia; and The Media in Zambia – Law and Practice.

He has previously worked as a State Advocate under the Attorney-General's Chambers as well as the Anti-Corruption Commission. He also worked as Legal Counsel in charge of Regulatory Affairs at the Zambia Telecommunications Company Limited.

He is formerly a lecturer and researcher in the School of Law of the University of Lusaka. He has also taught in the faculties of law at the University of Zambia, Zambian Open University, ZCAS University, National Institute of Public Administration, Mulungushi University and Zambia Air Force Centre for Advanced Learning. Subjects that he taught include law of torts, legal process, legal and academic writing, commercial law, criminal law, law of evidence, human rights law, jurisprudence and legal theory, legal aspects of international finance, medical law, local government law, administrative law and land law.

DEDICATION

To my Children: JJ, RJ, Nyasha, Lindi, Yabo and Thuli. For being my life, light and everything.

AND

To the memory of Jones Chama "Bashi Mwenya".

TABLE OF CONTENTS

CHAPTER

1

INTRODUCTION TO ECONOMIC CRIMINAL LAW

1.0 Introduction

This chapter will discuss the nature, types, effects as well as context of economic criminal law both at national and international level. Economic criminal law is that branch of criminal law that concerns itself with the criminalisation of economic crimes as well as their detection and prosecution. Due to the interdependence of state economies, this field of law has permeated all borders and is seen as an international rather than as a national scourge. It is noted that economic crime including money laundering is a part of the major transnational organized crime and that in order to combat economic crime, domestic, regional, and international law enforcement cooperation is required.[1] The Europol notes that the nature of financial crime requires working in collaboration amongst law enforcement and with organizations outside the law enforcement community.[2]

---

[1] https://www.unafei.or.jp/publications/pdf/RS_No67/No67_27RC_Group3.pdf [accessed on 30/11/2020 at 12:40 PM]

[2] https://www.interpol.int/en/Crimes/Financial-crime/Our-role-in-fighting-financial-crime [accessed 30/11/2020 at 3:20 PM]

1.1 Nature and types of economic crimes

It is difficult to give an exact definition of what an economic crime is but a list of activity may be used to provide the context of what the phenomena is.[3] Economic crime covers a wide range of offenses, from financial crimes committed by banks, tax evasion, illicit capital heavens, money laundering, crimes committed by public officials (like bribery, embezzlement, traffic of influences, etc.) among many others.[4] According to Eherb Edelhertz economic crime is an illegal act or series of acts committed by nonphysical means and by concealment or guile, to obtain money or property, to avoid the payment or loss of money or property, or to obtain business or personal advantage.[5]

The Eleventh United Nations (UN) Congress on Crime Prevention and Criminal Justice noted that the term "economic and financial crime" refers broadly to any non-violent crime that results in a financial loss, even though at times such losses may be hidden or not socially perceived as such. It was the Congress' finding that such crimes thus

---

[3] Council of Europe Committee of Ministers, 'Recommendation No. R (81) 12 of the Committee of Ministers to Member States on Economic Crime,' Adopted by the Committee of Ministers on 25 June 1981 at the 335th meeting of the Ministers' Deputies available at https://rm.coe.int/16806cb4f0

[4] http://www.cipce.org.ar/en/what-is-economic-crime [accessed on 30/11/2020 tat 12:51 PM]

[5] S Dinitz, 'Economic Crime" in Simha F Landau and Leslie Sebba (1977). Criminology in Perspective - Essays in honor of Israel Drapkin. New York: Lexington Books available at https://www.ncjrs.gov/App/Publications/abstract.aspx?ID=45546

include a broad range of illegal activities and that nevertheless, the category of "economic crime" escapes easy description and its exact conceptualization remains a challenge.[6] There are a number of types of economic crimes recognised at both national and international law. The following are the major types of economic crimes to be discussed in this book:

- corruption, bribery and racketeering
- terrorism financing
- customs related offences
- money laundering
- tax related offences
- fraud
- electronic crime
- bribery and corruption
- market abuse and insider dealing
- information security

1.2 International context and effects of economic crimes

The nature of economic crimes is that it has made the phenomena global and international instead of one that is a concern of individual countries. It has been observed that

---

[6] Eleventh United Nations (UN) Congress on Crime Prevention and Criminal Justice, 'Economic and financial crimes: challenges to sustainable development: Working paper prepared by the Secretariat,' available at https://www.unodc.org/pdf/WP%20on%20item%206%20V0581301%20in%20English.doc

the perpetration of economic and financial crimes has a number of direct costs in developing countries.[7] Most notably, such crimes often have a serious impact on the poor, given that they result in the diversion of resources away from government. In developing countries, ordinary citizens, with few savings or resources to absorb the consequences, are, for example, victimized by small-scale fraud at a considerably higher level than their counterparts in developed countries.[8] The United Kingdom (UK) Policy Paper on Economic Crime Plan, 2019 to 2022 speaks to this when it states that:

> Economic crime is a significant threat to the security and the prosperity of the UK [and the word]. It impacts all of our society, including our citizens, private sector businesses and the government. Fraud is now one of the most common crimes in the UK, with one in fifteen people falling victim a year. Money laundering enables criminals to profit from some of the most damaging crimes. Bribery and corruption undermine fair competition and are barriers to economic growth, especially in the developing world. Terrorist financing facilitates the atrocities we have suffered here in the UK as well as across Europe and the rest of the world. All economic crimes weaken people's faith in the

---

[7] id
[8] id

effectiveness of governmental and commercial organizations. To ensure the integrity of our financial system, protect our vulnerable people and communities, and attract business to the UK, we must do all in our power to combat economic crime.[9]

This was in relation to the UK but surely the truth of the statement above speaks on the effects of economic crimes as they relate to the whole world, Zambia inclusive.

1.3 Conclusion

This chapter has shown, albeit in brief, the scope and nature of economic crimes. It has been seen that economic crimes manifest themselves in various types such as corruption, bribery, money laundering and racketeering among others. In the same vein, it has been seen that economic crimes have a deleterious effect on the general socio-economic and human development. It was also seen that the fight against economic crimes require a global front as the phenomena has been globalised due to the nature of the world which is one global village and the advancement of technology.

---

[9] https://www.gov.uk/government/publications/economic-crime-plan-2019-to-2022/economic-crime-plan-2019-to-2022-accessible-version [accessed on 30/11/2020 at 3:27 PM]

CHAPTER

2

INSTITUTIONAL FRAMEWORK FOR COMBATING ECONOMIC CRIMES IN ZAMBIA

2.0 Introduction

This Chapter discusses the institutional framework established at national level in the combat of economic crimes. The chapter traces both the statutory mandate from where a particular institution draws its power as well as the duties, functions and roles of that particular institution. These institutions are collectively called the "intelligence community" in the combat of economic crimes.

2.1 Anti-Corruption Commission

The Anti-Corruption Commission (ACC) is one of the investigative commissions in line with Article 235 of the Constitution of Zambia, Chapter 1 of the Laws of Zambia.[10] It is established by the Anti-Corruption Act No. 3 of 2012 (hereinafter referred to as the "AC Act"). Section 4 of the AC Act provides that:

> The Anti-Corruption Commission continued

---

[10] As amended by Act No. 2 of 2016

under the repealed Act shall continue to exist as if established under this Act, and shall be a body corporate with perpetual succession and a common seal, capable of suing and of being sued in its corporate name and with power, subject to this Act, to do all such acts and things as a body corporate may, by law, do or perform.

The ACC was originally established under the Corrupt Practices Act of 1980.[11]It was continued under the Anti-Corruption Commission, Chapter 91 of the Laws of Zambia[12] and the Anti-Corruption Act No. 38 of 2010. Section 4 (1) of the ACC Act, Chapter 91 of the Laws of Zambia provided as follows:

There is hereby established the Anti-Corruption Commission which shall be a body corporate with perpetual succession and a common seal, capable of suing and being sued in its corporate name, and with power, subject to the provisions of this Act, to do all such things as a body corporate may, by law do or perform.

The ACC was continued under sections 4 (1) of the Anti-Corruption Act No. 38 of 2011 and section 4 (1) of the AC Act. The main function of the ACC is to spearhead and lead the fight against corruption in Zambia. Section 6 of

---

[11] Act No.14 of 1980
[12] Act No. 46 of 1996

the AC Act provides the functions of the ACC and this provision states that:

(1) The functions of the Commission are to—

(a) prevent and take necessary and effective measures for the prevention of corruption in public and private bodies, including, in particular, measures for—

(i) examining the practices and procedures of public and private bodies in order to facilitate the discovery of opportunities of corrupt practices and secure the revision of methods of work or procedures which in the opinion of the Commission, may be prone or conducive to corrupt practices;

(ii) advising public bodies and private bodies on ways and means of preventing corrupt practices, and on changes in methods of work or procedures of such public bodies and private bodies compatible with the effective performance of their duties, which the Commission considers necessary to reduce the likelihood of the occurrence of corrupt practices;

(iii) disseminating information on the evil and dangerous effects of corrupt practices on society;

(iv) creation of committees in institutions for monitoring corruption in the institution; and

(v) enlisting and fostering public confidence and support against corrupt practices;

(b) initiate, receive and investigate complaints of alleged or suspected corrupt practices, and, subject to the directions of the Director of Public Prosecutions, prosecute—

(i) offences under this Act; and

(ii) such other offence under any other written law as may have come to the notice of the Commission during the investigation of an offence under this Act:

Provided that nothing in this paragraph shall be considered as precluding any public prosecutor from prosecuting, subject to the directions of the Director of Public Prosecutions, any offence under this Act which has come to the notice of the police during investigation of an offence under any written law;

(c) investigate any conduct of any public officer which, the Commission has reasonable grounds to believe may be connected with, or conducive to, corrupt practices;

(d) be the lead agency in matters of corruption;

(e) co-ordinate or co-operate, as applicable, with other institutions authorised to investigate, prosecute, prevent and combat corrupt practices so as to implement an integrated approach to the eradication of corruption;

(f) consult, co-operate and exchange information with appropriate bodies of other countries that are authorised to conduct inquiries or investigations in relation to corrupt practices;

(g) adopt and strengthen mechanisms for educating the public to respect the public good and public interest and, in particular —

(i) create awareness in the fight against corruption and related offences;

(ii) develop educational and other programmes for the sensitisation of the media;

(iii) promote an environment for the respect of ethics; and

(iv) disseminate information and sensitise the public on the negative effects of corruption and related offences; and

(h) do all such things as are incidental or conducive to the attainment of its functions.

In sum, the functions of the ACC may be grouped into three categories: one, to investigate and prosecute cases of suspected corruption; two, to conduct public sensitization on the dangers of corruption and foster public support in the fight against corruption; and three, to put in place mechanisms for preventing the corruption scourge.[13]

2.2 Drug Enforcement Commission

The Drug Enforcement Commission (DEC), alongside the ACC and Anti-Financial and Economic Crimes Commission, is an investigative commission established by the Constitution.[14] There appears to be a conflict between Article 135 of the Constitution which establishes DEC as an independent commission and section 4 (2) of the Narcotic Drugs and Psychotropic Substances Act, Chapter 96 of the Laws of Zambia which provides that DEC shall be a department in the Ministry responsible for Home Affairs and shall be under the control and supervision of the Minister responsible for home affairs. In line with Article 1 (1) of the Constitution, section 4 seems to be *prima facie* null and void as it appears to have some

---

[13] http://www.acc.gov.zm/mandate/ [accessed 30/11/2020 at 4:17 PM]

[14] Article 135 of the Constitution of Zambia, Chapter 1 of the Laws of Zambia as amended by Act No. 2 of 2016; Suffice it to add that the Anti-Financial and Economic Crimes Commission is not yet in existence as at the publication of this book

inconsistencies with the Constitution.[15]

The DEC is established under section 4 of the Narcotic Drugs and Psychotropic Substances Act which provides that:

(1) The Drug Enforcement Commission established under the Dangerous Drugs (Forfeiture of Property) (Special Organisations) (Drug Enforcement Commission) Regulations, 1989, is hereby continued as if established under this Act.

(2) The Commission shall be a department in the Ministry responsible for Home Affairs and shall be under the control and supervision of the Minister responsible for Home Affairs.

(3) The provisions of the First Schedule shall apply to the Commission.

The main functions of DEC are to investigate drug and money laundering offences.[16] The DEC has the following functions in line with section 5 which provides that:

The functions of the Commission shall be to-

---

[15] Article 1 (1) of the Constitution provides that "This Constitution is the supreme law of the Republic of Zambia and any other written law, customary law and customary practice that is inconsistent with its provisions is void to the extent of the inconsistency" and this provision was construed in the cases of Thomas Mumba v The People (1984) ZR 38; Godfrey Malembeka (suing as Executive Director of Prisons Care and Counselling Association) v Attorney General and another Selected Judgment No. 34 of 2017 (CC); and Christine Mulundika and 7 Others v The People SCZ Judgment No. 25 of 1995

[16] http://www.deczambia.gov.zm/ [accessed 30/11/2020 at 4:28 PM]

(a) collect, collate and disseminate information on narcotic drugs and psychotropic substances;

(b) receive and investigate any complaint of alleged or suspected breach of this Act and, subject to the directives of the Director of Public Prosecutions, prosecute for offences under this Act;

(c) address and advise Government Ministries and departments, public bodies, companies, institutions, statutory bodies and corporations on ways and means of preventing prohibited activities relating to narcotic drugs and psychotropic substances and suggest measures, procedures or methods of work compatible with the proper performance of their duties which, in the opinion of the Commission, would reduce prohibited activities relating to narcotic drugs and psychotropic substances;

(d) disseminate information intended to educate the public on the evils and dangerous effects of abusing drugs or psychotropic substances and the effect of dealing in property acquired from drug trafficking; and

(e) enlist and foster public support against the abuse of drugs or psychotropic substances and, in this connection, liaise with similar authorities outside Zambia.

2.3 Anti-Money Laundering Authority

The Anti-Money Laundering Authority (AMLA) is composed of the following members appointed by the Minister: the Attorney-General, who is the chairperson; Inspector-General of the Zambia Police Service; the Commissioner;[17] the Director-General of the Anti-Corruption Commission; the Governor, Bank of Zambia; the Commissioner-General, Zambia Revenue Authority; and the two other persons.[18] The functions of the AMLA is firstly to provide general or specific policy directives to the Commissioner which directives the Commissioner is required to give effect.[19] The second function of the AMLA is to advise the Minister on measures required to prevent and detect money laundering in the Republic.[20]

Under the same Act, there is established the Anti-Money Laundering Investigations Unit (AMIU).[21] The AMIU comprises the Commissioner and such other officers as the Commissioner shall appoint.[22] The functions of the AMIU are to:

---

[17] Commissioner means the person appointed as Commissioner under the Narcotic Drugs and Psychotropic Substances Act as per section 2 of the Act
[18] Section of the Prohibition and Prevention of Money Laundering Act No. 14 of 2001
[19] Section 4
[20] id
[21] Section 5
[22] id

(a) to collect, evaluate, process and investigate financial information including that from regulated institutions and Supervisory Authorities, relating to financial and other business transactions suspected to be part of money laundering for the purpose of preventing and suppressing money laundering offences;[23]

(b) to conduct investigations and prosecutions of money laundering offences;

(c) to liaise with other law enforcement agencies in the conduct of investigations and prosecutions of money laundering offences;

(d) to supervise the reporting requirements and other administrative obligations imposed on regulated institutions and Supervisory Authorities under this Act;

(e) to assist, in developing, training programmes for use by regulated institutions

---

[23] " Supervisory Authority" means (a) the Bank of Zambia; (b) the Registrar of Building Societies appointed under the Building Societies Act; (c) the Registrar of Banks and Financial Institutions appointed under the Banking and Financial Services Act; (d) the Registrar of Co-operatives appointed under the Cooperatives Societies Act; (e) the Registrar of Insurance appointed under the Insurance Act; (f) the Commissioner appointed under the Securities and Exchange Commission Act; (g) the Registrar of Companies appointed under the Companies Act; (h) the Commissioner of Lands; (i) the Investment Board under the Investment Act; or (j) the licensing authority under the Casino Act; (k) any other authority which may be established by law as a Supervisory Authority as per section 2 of the same Act

and Supervisory Authorities in the implementation of this Act; and

(f) to cooperate withdraw enforcement agencies and institutions in other jurisdictions responsible for investigations and prosecution of money laundering offences.[24]

2.4 Financial Intelligence Centre

The Financial Intelligence Centre (FIC) was established by the Financial Intelligence Centre Act No. 46 of 2010 (hereinafter referred to as the "FIC Act").[25] Section 5 (1) of the FIC Act makes FIC the sole designated National Agency mandated to receive, request, analyse and disseminate disclosure of information concerning suspected money laundering, terrorist financing and other serious offences to competent authorities for investigations with the view of assisting with combatting money laundering, terrorist financing and other serious offences.[26] The functions of FIC are to:

(a) receive, request and analyse suspicious transaction reports required to be made under this Act or any other written law, including information from any foreign designated authority;

(b) analyse and evaluate suspicious transaction

---

[24] Section 6
[25] Section 3
[26] https://www.fic.gov.zm/about-us [accessed 30/11/2020 at 5:35 PM]

reports and information so as to determine whether there is sufficient basis to transmit reports for investigation by the law enforcement agencies or a foreign designated authority;

(c) disseminate information to law enforcement agencies, where there are reasonable grounds to suspect money laundering or financing of terrorism;

(d) provide information relating to suspicious transactions in accordance with this Act to any foreign designated authority, subject to such conditions as the Director may determine;

(e) provide information, advice and assistance to law enforcement agencies in furtherance of an investigation;

(f) enter into any agreement or arrangement, in writing, with a foreign designated authority which the Board considers necessary or desirable for the discharge or performance of its functions;

(g) conduct inquiries on behalf of foreign designated authorities and notify them of the outcome;

(h) inform the public and reporting entities of

their obligations and measures that have been or might be taken to detect, prevent and deter money laundering and financing of terrorism;

(i) access directly or indirectly, on a timely basis financial, administrative or law enforcement information, required for the better carrying out of its functions under this Act; and

(j) perform such other functions as are necessary to give effect to this Act.[27]

2.5 National Anti-Terrorism Centre

The National Anti-Terrorism Centre (NATC) is established under section 5 of the Anti-Terrorism and Non-Proliferation Act No. 6 of 2018 (hereinafter referred to as the "Anti-Terrorism Act") with the sole purpose of responsibility of enforcing the Act. The NATC is a unit based in the Ministry responsible for national security and is under the control and supervision of the Minister responsible for internal security (in this case home affairs).[28] The NATC is responsible for coordinating the prevention, detection, response to, mitigation and investigation of terrorists acts, financing of terrorism, proliferation, proliferation financing and threats to internal security.[29] Among other functions of the NATC include:

---

[27] Section 5 (2) as amended by Act No. 4 of 2016
[28] Section 5 (2)
[29] Section 6(1)

(a) draw up plans and coordinate actions for counter-terrorism acts, terrorism financing, proliferation and proliferation financing;

(b) integrate and analyse intelligence pertaining to terrorism, proliferation and proliferation financing;

(c) maintain a database of known and suspected terrorists and terrorist organisations, their networks, goals, strategies, capabilities, support and other relevant information;

(d) provide law enforcement agencies access to the intelligence support necessary to execute counterterrorism and proliferation plans and accomplish their assigned tasks;

(e) coordinate with investigation and intelligence agencies to ensure effective detection and prosecution of terrorism, terrorism financing, proliferation and proliferation financing;

(f) prepare regular threat assessment reviews and disseminate them to the appropriate levels in the Government;

(g) develop and promote the adoption of best practices for coordination of law enforcement agencies, government institutions and the general public in combating of terrorism; and

(h) enhance the State's capacity to—

(i) prevent the creation of safe havens for terrorists;

(ii) detect chemical, biological, radioactive or nuclear materials;

(iii) search, confiscate and establish safe control of chemical, biological, radioactive or nuclear materials;

(iv) account for, control and provide physical protection of chemical, biological, radioactive or nuclear threats;

(v) provide security of civilian and non-civilian institutions from chemical, biological, radioactive or nuclear threats;

(vi) respond to, mitigate and investigate chemical, biological, radioactive or nuclear incidents;

(vii) facilitate national, regional and global sharing of information for countering terrorism, terrorism financing, proliferation and proliferation financing;

(viii) ensure ratification and implementation of international conventions on terrorism and proliferation;

(ix) coordinate the implementation of the applicable United Nations Security Council Resolutions and other international conventions on terrorism;

(x) provide centralised services to law enforcement agencies, Government institutions and the general public in matters of national security or public interest in the following:

(A) forensic criminal investigations;

(B) scene of crime investigations;

(C) forensic accounting investigations;

(D) visual technical surveillance of public places to help in investigations of crime;

(E) laboratory analysis of chemical, biological, radioactive and nuclear materials, whether connected to crime or not; and

(F) maintenance of a general national database of suspected terrorists or terrorist organisations; and

(xi) facilitate or recommend appropriate training of security and defence personnel in countering terrorism.

The general policy direction of the NATC is the responsibility of the National Anti-Terrorism Committee which is appointed by the President.[30] The Committee is responsible for giving general or specific policy directives to the NATC regarding obligations and measures to be taken in the prevention, detection, and deterrence of the commission of terrorism acts, financing of terrorism, proliferation and proliferation financing; and to perform such other functions as are necessary to give effect to Anti-Terrorism Act.[31] It is comprised of the following members:

(a) the Director-General of the Zambia Security Intelligence Service who is the Chairperson;

(b) the Inspector-General of Police, who is the Vice Chairperson; and

(c) one representative each of—

(i) the Zambia Army;

(ii) the Zambia Air Force;

(iii) the Zambia National Service;

(iv) the Immigration Department;

(v) Financial Intelligence Centre;

(vi) Drug Enforcement Commission;

---

[30] Section 7
[31] Section 8

(vii) Attorney-General's Chambers; and

(viii) any other relevant institution as the President considers necessary for purposes of the Anti-Terrorism Act.[32]

2.6 Bank of Zambia

The Bank of Zambia (BoZ) is the central bank of the republic whose functions are to issue the currency of the Republic; determine monetary policy; and regulate banking and financial services, banks, financial and non-banking institutions, as prescribed.[33] Section 4 of the Bank of Zambia Act, Chapter 360 of the Laws of Zambia[34] (hereinafter referred to as the "BoZ Act") provides that:

> 4. (1) The Bank shall formulate and implement monetary and supervisory policies that will ensure the maintenance of price and financial systems stability so to promote balanced macro-economic development.
>
> (2) Without prejudice to the generality of subsection (1) and subject to the other provisions of this Act the Bank shall –
>
> (a) licence, supervise and regulate the activities of banks and financial institutions so as to

---

[32] Section 7 (1)

[33] Article 213 of the Constitution

[34] Act No. 43 of 1996; It also derives its mandate from the Banking and Financial Services Act No. 7 of 2017 and the Bank of Zambia (Amendment) Act No. 1 of 2013 among others

promote the safe, sound and efficient operations and development of the financial system;

(b) promote efficient payment mechanisms;

(c) issue notes and coins to be legal tender in the Republic and regulate all matters relating to the currency of the Republic;

(d) act as banker and fiscal agent to the Republic;

(e) support the efficient operation of the exchange system; and

(f) act as adviser to the Government on matters relating to economic and monetary management.

Arising from the above, the functions of BoZ are to:

- to ensure appropriate monetary policy formulation and implementation;
- provide banking services to Government , commercial banks and to act as Settlement Agent;
- to license, regulate and supervise banks and financial service institutions;
- to ensure a safe and sound financial system and;

- to manage the banking, currency and payment systems operations of the Bank of Zambia.[35]

It is from this mandate that the Central Bank has tentacles in as far as combating of economic crime is concerned. From its mandate under Article 213 (2) (c) and section 4 (2) (a) of the BoZ Act for example, BoZ has issued directives and regulations directly aimed at combating financial crimes such as money laundering and terrorist financing among others. The Bank of Zambia Anti-Money Laundering Directives, 2004[36] and the Bank of Zambia Anti-Money Laundering and Combating the Financing of Terrorism or Proliferation Directives, 2017[37] are examples of the overarching arm of the central bank in combating economic crimes.

2.7 Zambia Security Intelligence Service

The Zambia Security Intelligence Service (ZSIS), famously called the Office of the President (Special Division), is established under Article 193 (1) (b) as a national security service charged with:

(a) ensuring national security by undertaking

---

[35] See section 4 of the National Payment Systems Act No. 1 of 2007 where under subsection 1 it provides that "Notwithstanding any other law to the contrary, the Bank of Zambia shall be responsible for the implementation of this Act and shall exercise its powers in relation to payment systems in accordance with this Act"

[36] Issued under section 12(4) of the Prohibition and Prevention of Money Laundering Act No. 14 of 2001

[37] Issued under section 36(4) of the Financial Intelligence Centre Act Number 46 of 2010

security intelligence and counter intelligence;

(b) preventing a person from suspending, overthrowing or illegally abrogating this Constitution; and

(c) performing other functions as prescribed.[38]

The functions of the ZSIS are found in the Zambia Security Intelligence Service Act No. 14 of 1998 (hereinafter referred to as the "ZSIS Act"). It is through the collection of intelligence that the ZSIS are stakeholders in the combatting of economic crimes.[39]

2.8 Zambia Police Service

The Zambia Police Service is a national security service established under the Constitution of Zambia[40] with the mandate of preserving the peace, for the prevention and detection of crime, and for the apprehension of offenders against the peace.[41] The Zambia Police Service is constitutionally mandated to:

(a) protect life and property;

(b) preserve peace and maintain law and order;

---

[38] Article 193 (3)
[39] Section 2 of the Act defines "intelligence" as any information collected and processed by an intelligence officer which has a bearing on the security interests of the Republic
[40] Article 193 (1) (a)
[41] Section 5 of the Zambia Police Act, Chapter 107 of the Laws of Zambia

(c) ensure the security of the people;

(d) detect and prevent crime;

(e) uphold the Bill of Rights;

(f) foster and promote good relationships with the Defence Force, other national security services and members of society; and

(g) perform other functions as prescribed.[42]

The Zambia Police Service has specialised units specially established to combat economic crimes such as the Anti-Fraud Unit, Anti-Copper Theft Unit, Anti-Motor Vehicle Theft Unit and the Anti-Piracy Unit among others.

2.9 Zambia Revenue Authority

The Zambia Revenue Authority (ZRA) is established under the Zambia Revenue Authority Act, Chapter 321 of the Laws of Zambia (hereinafter referred to as the "ZRA Act"). ZRA is an amalgamation of two government departments into a semi-autonomous authority. By this Act, the Department of Taxes and the Department of Customs and Excise were merged and their functions transferred to the newly created ZRA.[43] ZRA is responsible for collecting revenue on behalf of the Government of the Republic of Zambia (GRZ) under the supervision of the

---

[42] Article 193 (2)
[43] Preamble to and section 3 of the Act

Minister responsible for finance.[44] ZRA's responsibilities include assessment and collection of taxes and duties, enforcement of relevant statutory provisions, facilitation of international trade, and advisory on aspects of tax policy.[45] It also controls the transit of goods and service into and from Zambia and has a presence at all points of entry and exit. The Authority is the frontrunner in the combat against economic crimes such as tax evasion, counterfeiting and piracy and smuggling among others.[46]

2.10   National Audit Office

The National Audit Office is established under section 4 of the Public Audit Act No. 29 of 2016. The functions of the National Audit Office are to:

(a) perform audits under the Public Finance Act, 2004,[47] and any other written law;

(b) recommend to the Commission the organisational structure and technical competencies required for the efficient and effective performance of its functions;

(c) recommend to the Commission the terms

---

[44]   https://offgrid.gov.zm/en/Directory/Details/fd55e848-08eb-48a5-a43b-029709691228#:~:text=ZRA's%20responsibilities%20include%20assessment%20and,on%20aspects%20of%20tax%20policy. [accessed 01/12/2020 at 9:04 AM]

[45] id

[46] ZRA draws its mandate from a plethora of statutes that include the Income Tax Act, Chapter 323 of the Laws of Zambia; Customs and Excise Act, Chapter 322 of the Laws of Zambia and the Property Transfer Tax Act, Chapter 340 of the Laws of Zambia among others

[47] Repealed and replaced by Public Finance Management Act No. 1 of 2018

and conditions of service of officers and other employees of the National Audit Office, other than the Auditor-General; and

(d) do such other things as are necessary or incidental to the performance of its functions under this Act.[48]

The National Audit Office is headed by the Auditor-General as established under Article 249 of the Constitution. The functions of the Auditor-General are:

(a) audit the accounts of—

(i) State organs, State institutions, provincial administration and local authorities; and

(ii) institutions financed from public funds;

(b) audit the accounts that relate to the stocks, shares and stores of the Government;

(c) conduct financial and value for money audits, including forensic audits and any other type of audit, in respect of a project that involves the use of public funds;

(d) ascertain that money appropriated by Parliament or raised by the Government and disbursed—

(i) has been applied for the purpose for which

---

[48] Section 5 of the Public Audit Act; see also Article 234 of the Constitution

it was appropriated or raised;

(ii) was expended in conformity with the authority that governs it; and

(iii) was expended economically, efficiently and effectively; and

(e) recommend to the Director of Public Prosecutions or a law enforcement agency any matter within the competence of the Auditor-General, that may require to be prosecuted.[49]

2.11 National Prosecution Authority

The National Prosecution Authority (NPA) is created under section of the National Prosecution Act No. 34 of 2010 (hereinafter referred to as the "NPA Act"). The NPA is headed by the Director of Public Prosecutions (DPP) who is a constitutional office holder as provided by Article 180 of the Constitution. The DPP is the chief prosecutor for the Government and head of the NPA[50] and the power to: one, institute and undertake criminal proceedings against a person before a court, other than a court-martial, for an offence alleged to have been committed by that person; two, take over and continue criminal proceedings instituted or undertaken by another person or authority; and three, discontinue, at any stage before judgment is delivered, criminal proceedings instituted or undertaken by

---

[49] Article 250 (1)
[50] Article 180 (3)

the Director of Public Prosecutions or another person or authority.[51]The NPA, under the direction of the DPP, is responsible for all prosecutions in this jurisdiction.

The functions of the DPP are outlined under section 8 of the NPA Act and include the following:

(a) institute and undertake criminal proceedings against any person before any court, other than a court martial, in respect of any offence alleged to have been committed by that person;

(b) take over and continue any such criminal proceedings as may have been instituted or undertaken by any other person or authority; and

(c) discontinue, at any stage before judgment is delivered, any criminal proceedings instituted or undertaken by the Director of Public Prosecutions or any other person or authority;

(d) set the qualification for the appointment of prosecutors;

(e) advise prosecutors on all matters relating to criminal offences;

(f) review a decision to prosecute, or not to

---

[51] Article 180 (4)

prosecute, any criminal offence;

(g) advise the Minister on all matters relating to the administration of criminal justice;

(h) liaise with the Chief State Advocate, the Deputy Chief State Advocates, the prosecutors, the legal profession and legal institutions in order to foster common practices and to promote co-operation in the handling of complaints in respect of the Authority;

(i) assist the Deputy Chief State Advocates and prosecutors in achieving the effective and fair administration of criminal justice;

(j) liaise with and assist the Attorney-General in matters of extradition and mutual legal assistance in criminal matters; and

(k) appoint such experts as are necessary to assist the Director of Public Prosecutions carry out any functions under this Act.[52]

2.12   Conclusion

This Chapter has discussed the main institutions present in this jurisdiction to detect and prosecute economic crimes. Each of the institutions, it has been seen, has a specific mandate in the fight against economic crimes but at the

---

[52] See Part V of the AC Act on the powers of the DPP

same time they complement each other and supplement the efforts of one another.

CHAPTER
3

LEGAL FRAMEWORK FOR COMBATING ECONOMIC CRIMES IN ZAMBIA

3.0 Introduction

This Chapter will discuss the various statutes available in this jurisdiction in the combat against economic crimes. These statutes are not in themselves comprehensive as there are many other statutory instruments and forms of delegated legislation that have been promulgated in the fight against the scourge.

3.1 Anti-Corruption Act

The AC Act is an Act enacted to continue the existence of the ACC and to provide for its powers and functions; provide for the prevention, detection, investigation, prosecution and punishment of corrupt practices and related offences based on the rule of law, integrity, transparency, accountability and management of public affairs and property; provide for the development, implementation and maintenance of coordinated anticorruption strategies through the promotion of public participation; provide for the protection of witnesses, experts, victims and other persons assisting the Commission; provide for nullification of corrupt transactions; provide for payment of compensation for damage arising out of corrupt activities; provide for the domestication of the United Nations Convention Against Corruption,[53] the African Union Convention on Preventing and Combating Corruption,[54] the Southern African Development Community Protocol Against Corruption[55] and other regional and international instruments on corruption to which Zambia is a party; repeal and replace the Anti-Corruption Act, 2010; and provide for matters connected with, or incidental to, the foregoing.[56]

Part III of the Act creates offences termed corrupt practices while Part IV guides on how investigations regarding corrupt practices may be undertaken. The powers of the DPP in relation to prosecution of corrupt practices are found under Part V while matters relating to production and tendering of evidence are provided for under Part VI of the Act.

3.2 Prohibition and Prevention of Money Laundering Act

The Prohibition and Prevention of Money Laundering Act (PPMLA) of 2001 is another major statute in the realm of

---

[53] Adopted by the United Nations General Assembly on 31st October 2003 by Resolution 58/4

[54] Adopted on 1st July , 2003

[55] Adopted on 14th August, 2001

[56] Preamble to Act No. 3 of 2012

economic crimes.[57] The PPMLA is an Act aimed at providing for the prohibition and prevention of money laundering; the constitution of the AMLA and the AMLIU; provision for the disclosure of information on suspicion of money laundering activities by Supervisory Authorities and regulated institutions; provision for the forfeiture of property of persons convicted of money laundering; to provision for international cooperation in investigations, prosecution and other legal processes of prohibiting and preventing money laundering; and provision for matters connected with or incidental to the foregoing.[58]

Part IV of the Act provides a list of offences termed money laundering offences while Part V gives a mechanism on the prevention of money laundering activities. Part VI provides for seizure and forfeiture of property in relation to money laundering.

3.3 Narcotic Drugs and Psychotropic Substances Act

The Narcotic Drugs and Psychotropic Substances Act (NDPSA) is an Act to continue the DEC; revise and consolidate the law relating to narcotic drugs and psychotropic substances; incorporate into Zambian law certain international Conventions governing illicit drugs and psychotropic substances; control the importation, exportation, production, possession, sale, distribution and use of narcotic drugs and psychotropic substances; provide for the seizure and forfeiture of property relating to, or

---

[57] Act No. 14 of 2001
[58] Preamble to the Act

connected with, unlawful activities involving narcotic drugs and psychotropic substances; repeal the Dangerous Drugs (Forfeiture of Property) Act, 1989; and provide for matters connected with or incidental to the foregoing.

Part II of the Act provides for offences and penalties such as trafficking in narcotic drugs or psychotropic substances prohibited; prohibition on importing or exporting narcotic drugs or psychotropic substances; prohibition on possession of narcotic drugs and psychotropic substances; cultivation of plants for narcotic or psychotropic purposes; and money laundering among others. Part IV contains provisions relating to investigation, arrest and seizure while Part V provides for matters relating to seizure and forfeiture of property relating to offences under the Act.

3.4 Anti-Terrorism and Non-Proliferation Act

The Anti-Terrorism and Non-Proliferation Act No. 6 of 2018 (hereinafter referred to as the "Anti-Terrorism Act") was promulgated in 2018 in order to repeal and replace the maiden anti-terrorism legislation in the name of the Anti-Terrorism Act of 2007.[59] The Anti-Terrorism Act is a piece of legislation that first and foremost establishes the National Anti-Terrorism Centre and provides for its functions.[60] It is also an Act aimed at preventing and

---

[59] Act No. 21 of 2007

[60] Preamble to the Act; see Musa Bah, 'A commentary on the confiscation regime in Zambia by way of review of the Forfeiture of Proceeds of Crime Act of 2010,' LLB Thesis (UNZA, 2013) and Cassandra Soko, 'An Evaluation of Zambia's Asset Recovery Laws,' LLM Thesis (University of the Western Cape, 2013) on the history of the Act

prohibiting the carrying out of terrorism financing and proliferation activities; provision of measures for the detection and prevention of terrorism and proliferation activities; provision of offences of proliferation and proliferation financing; domestication of international conventions and treaties on anti-terrorism and proliferation; repealing of the Anti-Terrorism Act, 2007; and provision of matters, connected with, or incidental to the foregoing.[61]

Part III of the Act provides for terrorist and proliferation offences such as prohibition of terrorism; prohibition of financing of terrorism; prohibition of proliferation; prohibition of proliferation financing; weapons, terrorism and proliferation training among others. Part VI has provisions relating to investigations, power to obtain financial information in relation to the Financial Intelligence Centre Act No. 26 of 2010 and obligations relating to the disclosure of information among others.

3.5 Forfeiture of Proceeds of Crime Act

The Forfeiture of Proceeds of Crime Act No. 19 of 2010 (hereinafter referred to as the "Forfeiture Act") is generally a piece of legislation that provides for the confiscation of the proceeds of crime and the deprivation of any person of any proceed, benefit or property derived from the commission of any serious offence or offences.[62] The Act also facilitates the tracing of any proceed, benefit and

---

[61] id
[62] Preamble

property derived from the commission of any serious offence or offences.[63] Most importantly, the Act domesticates the United Nations Convention against Corruption of 2003.

The Act also provides for obligations of financial institutions in that where a financial institution is required by law to release an original of a document before the end of the minimum retention period applicable to the document, the financial institution must retain a complete copy of the document until the period has ended or the original document is returned, whichever occurs first.[64] Section 71 of the Act also provides for the offence of possession of property suspected of being proceeds of crime.[65] Part VI establishes the Forfeited Assets Fund.

3.6 Financial Intelligence Centre Act

The Financial Intelligence Centre Act[66] is an Act as seen in the preceding Chapters that establishes the Financial Intelligence Centre (FIC) and provides for its functions and powers. The Act also provides for the duties of supervisory authorities and reporting entities as well as for matters connected with, or incidental to, the foregoing.[67] Part III of the Act provides for offences relating to prevention of money laundering terrorist financing and other serious

---

[63] id

[64] Section 66

[65] See The People v Austin Chisangu Liato (Appeal No. 291/2014)

[66] No. 46 of 2010

[67] Preamble

offences such as establishment of anonymous accounts. The Act also requires that reporting entities have in place KYC (Know Your Customer), due diligence, reporting of suspicious transactions, record keeping and training protocols among others.[68]

3.7 Public Interest Disclosure (Protection of Whistleblowers) Act

The Public Interest Disclosure (Protection of Whistleblowers) Act No. 4 of 2010 is an Act that provides for the disclosure of conduct adverse to the public interest in the public and private sectors; provides for a framework within which public interest disclosures shall be independently and rigorously dealt with; provides for procedures in terms of which employees in both the private and the public sectors may disclose information regarding unlawful or irregular conduct by their employers or other employees in the employ of their employers; aimed at safeguarding the rights, including employment rights, of persons who make public interest disclosures; and provide for a framework within which persons who make a public interest disclosure shall be protected.[69] Parts V and VI of the Act provides for the protection against reprisals for disclosing of information in public interest.

---

[68] Section 2 of the Financial Intelligence Centre (Amendment) Act No. 4 of 2016 defines a reporting entity to mean— (a) an institution regulated by a supervisory authority; or (b) an institution or designated non-financial business or profession supervised by the Centre pursuant to section five.
[69] Preamble to the Act

3.8 Mutual Legal Assistance in Criminal Matters Act

The Mutual Legal Assistance in Criminal Matters Act, Chapter 98 of the Laws of Zambia is an Act that provides for the implementation of treaties for mutual legal assistance in criminal matters and to provide for matters connected with or incidental to the foregoing.[70] This enables cooperation with other countries as the nature of economic crimes is that it is global and requires interdependence among countries.

3.9 Plea Negotiations and Agreements Act

The Plea Negotiations and Agreements Act No. 20 of 2010 is a statute that provides for plea negotiations and agreements. A plea negotiation means any negotiation carried out between an accused person or the accused person's legal representative, and a public prosecutor in relation to the accused person pleading guilty to a lesser offence than the offence charged or to one of multiple charges in return for any concession or benefit in relation to which charges are to be proceeded with.[71] A Plea agreement means an agreement made pursuant to section 4 of the Act;[72] that is to say an agreement as a result of a plea negotiation.[73] This Act may help avoid a protracted and expensive litigation in that the accused may bargain and get a lesser sentence for cooperating with the state.

---

[70] Preamble to the Act
[71] Section 2; see also section 4
[72] Section 2
[73] See section 7

3.10   Non-Governmental Organizations' Act

The Non-Governmental Organizations' Act No. 16 of 2009 is an Act that provides, *inter alia*, for the co-ordination and registration of non-governmental organisations.[74] Most importantly, it must be noted that Non-Governmental Organisations (NGOs) have time and again been used as vehicles for commission of economic offences such as money laundering. Their registration helps in the monitoring not only of the NGOs but also of the persons behind those entities.

3.11 Penal Code Act

The Penal Code Act, Chapter 87 of the Laws of Zambia as the name suggests is a Code that contains a list of offences in this jurisdiction. It is a Code of substantive criminal law with its counterpart, the Criminal Procedure Code, Chapter 88 of the Laws of Zambia, containing the procedural criminal law of this jurisdiction. The following are the cardinal provisions relating to economic criminal law in this jurisdiction:

- Offences relating to property under Division V
- Malicious injuries to property under Division VI
- Forgery, coining, counterfeiting and similar offences under Division VII

---

[74] Preamble to the Act

3.12 Customs and Excise Act

The Customs and Excise Act, Chapter 322 of the Laws of Zambia and other related Acts seek to combat activities that may undermine the revenue collection capacity of the Republic. Enforced by ZRA with the help of the Zambia Police service at times, this and other related Acts provide for offences such as those under Part XII of this Act:

- False statements by persons arriving in Zambia
- False invoices, false representation and forgery
- Possession of blank invoice
- Obstruction of officers
- Removing, altering, or defacing marks or seals
- Certain responsibilities of master, pilot, or person in charge of vehicle
- Removing or breaking locks placed on warehouse
- Failure to make full declaration of sealable goods
- Bribery, collusive seizure or agreement not to seize
- Smuggling
- Importation of prohibited or restricted goods to be an offence
- Miscellaneous offences
- Warehousing irregularities
- Offences by licensed manufacturer
- Offences relating to the use of ships, aircraft, or vehicles
- Concealed goods

- Forfeited packages, containers, or utensils
- Substitution of other goods for goods actually liable to seizure
- Vehicles carrying goods liable to forfeiture
- Ships, aircraft, or vehicles adapted for smuggling liable to forfeiture
- Power of officer to seize goods
- Pest infected or harmful goods[75]

3.13   National Payment Systems Act

The object of the National Payment Systems Act No. 1 of 2007 is to provide for the management, administration, operation, supervision and regulation of payment, clearing and settlement systems; to empower the BoZ to develop and implement payment, clearing and settlement systems policy so as to promote efficiency, stability and safety of the Zambian financial system; and to provide for matters connected with or incidental to the foregoing.[76] The power to enforce the provisions of this Act lies with the BoZ.[77] Section 5 of the Act provides that:

> (1) The Bank of Zambia shall regulate and oversee the operations of payment systems in order to ensure the integrity, effectiveness, efficiency, competitiveness and security of the payment systems so as to promote the

---

[75] See also Part X of the Income Tax Act, Chapter 323 of the Laws of Zambia on other offences
[76] Preamble to the Act
[77] Section 4 (1)

stability and safety of the Zambian financial system.

(2) The Bank of Zambia may, for the effective performance of its functions, under subsection (1), designate a particular payment system or such other payment systems as it considers necessary for purposes of this Act.

(3) Without prejudice to the generality of subsection (1) and subject to this Act, the Bank of Zambia may —

(a) regulate entry criteria of participants to a payment system;

(b) issue and vary guidelines to be followed by participants with respect to payment orders;

(c) prescribe rules and arrangements relating to the operation of payment systems and in particular provide for—

(i) netting agreements;

(ii) risk-sharing and risk-control mechanisms;

(iii) finality of settlement and finality of payment;

(iv) the nature of financial arrangements among participants;

(v) the operational systems and financial

soundness of a clearing house; and

(vi) such other matters pertaining to systemic risk; and

(d) give such directives to participants as may be necessary to ensure the integrity, effectiveness, efficiency or security of the payment system.

The gist of the role of the Act and the responsibility shouldered on the BoZ is to promote efficiency, stability and safety of the Zambian financial system. Thus, offences have been created under the Act such as those involving issuing of false documents (section 31), use of misleading names (section 32) and issuance of cheques on insufficiently funded accounts with intent to defraud (section 33).

3.14   Public Procurement Act

The Public Procurement Act No. 12 of 2008 is an Act mainly to revise the law relating to procurement so as to ensure transparency and accountability in public procurement; regulate and control practices relating to public procurement in order to promote the integrity of, fairness and public confidence in, the procurement process.[78] It seeks to outlaw the presence of corrupt, coercive and collusive practices in the procurement process which practices may have deleterious effects on the

---

[78] Preamble to the Act

national treasury and quality of the public goods and services procured.[79] It also proscribes fraudulent practices in the procurement process.[80]

The Act also establishes the Zambia Public Procurement Authority (ZPPA) which is an independent regulatory body with responsibility for policy, regulation, standard setting, compliance and performance monitoring, professional development and information management and dissemination in the field of public procurement.[81] The functions of ZPPA as espoused under section 6 are to:

(a) regulate the procurement of goods, works and services by procuring entities and ensure transparency and accountability in public procurement;

(b) monitor compliance with this Act and the procurement performance of the procuring entities and make recommendations to the Minister on the performance and functioning

---

[79] By section 2 of the Act "corrupt practice" means the offering, giving, receiving or soliciting, directly or indirectly, of anything of value to influence the action of a public officer in the procurement process or in contract execution; "coercive practices" means harming or threatening to harm, directly or indirectly, a person, or a person's property, to influence that person's participation in a procurement process or affect the execution of a contract; and "collusive practices" means a scheme or arrangement between two or more bidders, with or without the knowledge of the procuring entity, designed to establish bid prices at artificial, non-competitive levels.

[80] Section 2 of the Act defines "fraudulent practice" to mean a misrepresentation or omission of facts in order to influence a procurement process or the execution of a contract.

[81] Sections 5 and 6

of the public procurement system;

(c) issue standard bidding documents and other standard procurement documents for use by procuring entities;

(d) advise the Government and procuring entities on procurement policy and other matters relating to public procurement;

(e) consider applications for deviations to public procurement processes, methods and rules and for the accreditation of alternative procurement systems;

 (f) commission and undertake in v e s t i g a t i o n s in public procurement matters and institute procurement audits;

(g) promote economy, efficiency and maximum competition to ensure value for money in the use of public funds;

(h) promote private sector participation, through fair and non-discriminatory treatment of bidders;

(i) formulate preference and reservation schemes to promote the economic development of citizen bidder and suppliers in collaboration with the appropriate Government institutions;

(j) maintain a register of bidders and suppliers who are suspended from participating in public procurement;

(k) coordinate and promote capacity-building and professional development in the public procurement system;

(l) organise and maintain systems for the management of procurement data, statistics and information and for the publication of data on public procurement opportunities, contract awards and other information of public interest; and

(m) do all such other acts and things as are incidental to the foregoing or conducive to the attainment of the objectives of the Authority.

In sum, the Act provides a framework of rules, systems and processes for the procurement process of public goods and services. It helps in the elimination of conduct that may be detrimental to the economic wellbeing of the Republic.

3.15 Public Finance Management Act

The Public Finance Management Act No.1 of 2018 (hereinafter referred to as the "Public Finance Act") repealed and replaced the Public Finance Act No. 15 of 2004. The purpose of the Act is to provide for an institutional and regulatory framework for management of public funds; the strengthening of accountability, oversight, management and control of public funds in the public financial management framework; responsibilities and fiduciary duties of controlling officers and Controlling bodies; enhancement of cash management systems to ensure efficient and effective utilisation of cash for the Government; the processes for efficient production of the Financial Report for the Republic; the management and control of public assets and stores; and matters connected with, or incidental, to, the foregoing.[82]

Part IV of the Act deals with financial misconduct by officers, committees and office holders while section 82 of the Act provides for offences and provides as follows:

> (1) A person commits an offence if that person, wilfully and without lawful authority—
>
> (a) opens or causes to be opened any bank account for public or official use;
>
> (b) borrows money on behalf of a public body, or repays or converts an existing loan;
>
> (c) issues public securities, or varies the terms and conditions of the issued public security;
>
> (d) lends money or any assets of a public body;

---

[82] Preamble to the Act

(e) issues guarantees or indemnities on behalf of a public body;

(f) issues securities for loans made to the public body;

(g) disposes of, pledges, or encumbers property of a public body;

(h) refuses or omits to pay any public money into a public or official bank account as may be required;

(i) incurs unauthorised expenditures or makes unauthorised commitments;

(j) fails to provide by the due date, any information the Secretary to the Treasury may reasonably require under this Act;

(k) fails to provide any information that the Auditor-General, Accountant General, Controller of Internal Audit or a person authorised by the Auditor-General, Accountant General or Controller of Internal Audit may reasonably require under this Act;

(l) fails to provide, or obstructs access to any item required under this Act;

(m) fails to keep proper records or conceals or destroys information that is required to be recorded by this Act;

(n) makes any statement or declaration, or gives any information or document, required under this Act, knowing it to be false or misleading;

(o) alters or divulges data in electronic or other form; or

(p) fails to comply with any requirement of this Act or to execute a duty or function imposed on that person under this Act.

(2) A person who steals public funds or public stores, or public property commits an offence.

(3) A person who commits an offence under subsection (1) is liable, on conviction, to a fine not exceeding five hundred thousand penalty units, or a term of imprisonment not exceeding five years, or to both.

(4) Subject to the other provisions of this Act, an offence under this part shall be inquired into, tried, and otherwise dealt with in accordance with the Criminal Procedure Code, the Penal Code and any other written law.

(5) Nothing in this Act prejudices, limits or restricts—

(a) the operation of any other law which

provides for the forfeiture of property or the imposition of penalties or fines;

(b) the remedies available to the State apart from this Act, for the enforcement of its rights and the protection of its interests; or

(c) any power of search or any power to seize or to detain property which is exercisable by a police officer apart from this Act.

3.17 Conclusion

This Chapter has traversed the various legal instruments that govern the arena of economic crimes. It has been shown, though not conclusively, that the combat of economic crimes is broader and involves numerous pieces of legislation.

CHAPTER

4

CORRUPTION AND RELATED OFFENCES

4.0 Introduction

Corruption and related offences are the most prominent form of economic crimes in Zambia as many parts of the world. Many of these crimes are loosely termed corruption but it is important to note that they are significantly different from each other. This chapter will traverse the crime of corruption and other related offences as enunciated under the AC Act and international instruments.

4.1 Corruption

Reconstruing Corruption

The word "corruption" is derived from the Lain word *'corruptus'* meaning to break. Its derivation emphasises the destructive effect of corruption on the fabric of society and the fact that its popular meaning encompasses all those situations where agents and public officers break the confidence entrusted to them.[83] Transparency International

---

[83] Nicholls, C. et al (2011). Corruption and Misuse of Public Office, 2nd edn., Oxford: Oxford University Press at p.1

(TI), a non-profit non-governmental organization whose main objective is to take action to combat global corruption with civil societal anti-corruption measures and to prevent criminal activities arising from corruption, simply defines corruption as 'the abuse of entrusted power for private gain.'[84] This definition, Nicholls, QC *et al* note has the advantage of simplicity (although it does not include bribery which occurs wholly in the private sector) and, arguably, it embraces both offences of corruption strictly so-called, such as bribery, and related offences such as misconduct in public office, extortion, embezzlement, fraud, and theft, which are distinct offences, albeit usually committed in the course of corruption.[85]

Attempts to define corruption internationally

The African Union Convention on Preventing and Combating Corruption (hereinafter referred to as the "AU Convention") defines corruption as acts and practices including related offences proscribed in the Convention.[86] This definition is not helpful itself but it makes clear that corruption goes beyond the payment or receipt of bribes, and in essence, covers a range of situations, which Hatchard include:

(i) Bribery and 'kickbacks' that is the practice of paying a percentage of a particular contract to the

---

[84] https://www.transparency.org/en/what-is-corruption [Accessed on 30/12/2020 at 10:22 AM]
[85] Corruption and Misuse of Public Office, 2nd edn at pp.2-3
[86] Article 1

public official: under such euphemisms as 'consultancy fees' or 'facilitation fees';

(ii) Abuse of office including nepotism and cronyism;

(iii) Trading in influence: this focusses on the influence peddlers who cannot take decisions themselves but who are in the 'neighbourhood of power' and misuse their real or alleged influence on other persons to seek to obtain advantages for others;

(iv) Theft/looting of state assets; and

(v) Extortion: this relies on coercion, such as the use or threat of violence or the exposure of damaging information, to induce cooperation.[87]

The Southern African Development Community Protocol Against Corruption (hereinafter referred to as the "SADC Protocol") defines corruption to include bribery or any other behaviour in relation to persons entrusted with responsibilities in the public and private sectors which violates their duties as public officials, private employees, independent agents or other relationships of that kind and aimed at obtaining undue advantage of any kind or themselves or others.[88] The said Article on the definition of corruption refers us to Article III which lists acts of corruption as follows:

i. the solicitation or acceptance, directly or indirectly, by a public official, of any article of monetary value, or

---

[87] Hatchard, J (2014). Combating Corruption: Legal Approaches to Supporting Good Governance and Integrity in Africa. Cheltenham: Edward Elgar Publishing Limited at pp.14-15

[88] Article I

other benefit, such as a gift, favour, promise or advantage for himself or herself or for another person or entity, in exchange for any act or omission in the performance of his or her public functions;

ii. the offering or granting, directly or indirectly, by a public official, of any article of monetary value, or other benefit, such as a gift, favour, promise or advantage for himself or herself or for another person or entity, in exchange for any act or omission in the performance of his or her public functions;

iii. any act or omission in the discharge of his or her duties by a public official for the purpose of illicitly obtaining benefits for himself or herself or for a third party;

iv. the diversion by a public official, for purposes unrelated to those for which they were intended, for his or her own benefit or that of a third party of any movable or immovable property, monies or securities belonging to the State, to an independent agency, or to an individual, that such official received by virtue of his or her position for purposes of administration, custody or for other reasons;

v. the offering or giving, promising, solicitation or acceptance, directly or indirectly, of any undue advantage to or by any person who directs or works for, in any capacity, a private sector entity, for himself or herself or for anyone else, for him or her to act, or refrain from acting, in breach of his or her duties;

vi. the offering, giving, solicitation or acceptance directly or indirectly, or promising of any undue advantage to or by any person who asserts or confirms that he or she is able to exert any improper influence over the decision making of any person performing functions in the public or private sector in consideration thereof, whether the undue advantage is for himself or herself or for anyone else, as well as the request, receipt or the acceptance of the offer or the promise of such an advantage, in consideration of the influence, whether or not the influence is exerted or whether or not the supposed influence leads to the intended result;

vii. the fraudulent use or concealment of property derived from any of the acts referred to in [the] Article; and

viii. participation as a principal, co-principal, agent, instigator, accomplice or accessory after the fact, or in any other manner, in the commission or attempted commission of, in any collaboration or conspiracy to commit, any of the acts referred to in [the] Article.

Corruption under the AC Act

Corruption in this jurisdiction means soliciting,[89] accepting, obtaining, giving, promising or offering of gratification by way of a bribe or other personal temptation or inducement or the misuse or abuse of a public office or authority for private advantage or benefit through bribery, extortion, influence peddling, nepotism, fraud, rushed trials, and electoral malpractices.[90] Section 3 of the AC Act provides that:

> *"corrupt" means the soliciting, accepting, obtaining, giving, promising or offering of a gratification by way of a bribe or other personal temptation or inducement, or the misuse or abuse of a public office for advantage or benefit for oneself or another person, and "corruption" shall be construed accordingly.*

Corruption categorized

Corruption can be defined and categorized in different ways. The most common types or categories of corruption are supply versus demand corruption, grand versus petty corruption, conventional versus unconventional corruption and public versus private corruption.[91] There are other categories or ways of describing corruption, such as "systemic" versus "individual" or "isolated," corruption by "commission" versus by "omission," by the degree of coercion used to perform the illegal act, and the type of benefit provided.[92] This part will concentrate on grand corruption, petty corruption and systemic corruption.

- ▪ *Grand Corruption*

The term 'grand corruption' is used to describe cases where

---

[90] GRZ (2009). National Anti-Corruption Policy, 2009. Lusaka: Cabinet Office
[91] https://www.publicsafety.gc.ca/cnt/rsrcs/pblctns/rgnzd-crm-brf-48/rgnzd-crm-brf-48-en.pdf [Accessed 30/12/2020 at 11:40 AM]
[92] id

massive personal wealth is acquired from States by senior officials using corrupt means and it arises mostly where high officials have power over the granting of large public contracts and a local agent receives a commission if the transaction is won.[93] It has three main criteria: size, immediacy of its rewards, and mystification; the more technical and complicated a transaction the less likely it is that questions will be asked.[94] As stated above, it involves higher ranking government officials and elected officials who exploit opportunities that are presented through government work and is more often the result of bribes offered or paid in connection with larger scale government projects, such as infrastructure and construction projects.[95]

- *Petty Corruption*

Petty corruption is sometimes equated with "bureaucratic corruption," which implies involvement of public administration officials and non-elected officials.[96] Some examples of the use of petty corruption include bribes paid to enforcement officials, customs personnel, health service providers, and other government officials.[97] It is used to distinguish between grand corruption practised by Heads of States and Governments, Government Ministers, and senior officials, and the kind of corruption which, for

---

[93] Corruption and Misuse of Public Office, 2nd edn at p.3
[94] id
[95]   https://www.publicsafety.gc.ca/cnt/rsrcs/pblctns/rgnzd-crm-brf-48/rgnzd-crm-brf-48-en.pdf [Accessed 30/12/2020 at 11:40 AM]
[96] id
[97] id

example, magistrates and judges are subject, due to inadequate remuneration and facilities.[98] The term is often used to describe 'facilitation' or 'grease payments' sought by officials for services the public are entitled to free of charge, for example, payments to customs officers to pass goods through a border, to immigration officers to have travel documents accepted, to medical staff to receive prescription drugs or other benefits, payments for fictitious services, or to avoid prosecution for traffic offences, real or imaginary.[99]

- *Systemic Corruption*

This is institutionalised or entrenched corruption which is usually brought about, encouraged or promoted by the system itself. It occurs where bribery on a large scale is routine and its causes are usually brought about by inefficiency, inadequacy, or undue laxity in the system. Institutionalised corruption is visible in this country especially among police officers, judiciary officers and those at the ministry of lands.[100]

Types of corruption under the AC Act

The AC Act has different provisions relating to corruption in this jurisdiction which we can term as types of

---

[98] Corruption and Misuse of Public Office, 2nd edn at p.3

[99] Evidence to the British Parliamentary Select Committee on International Development by Transparency International on 4th April 2001

[100] See MLM Mbao, 'Prevention and combating of corruption in Zambia,' The Comparative and International Law Journal of Southern Africa, Vol. 44, No. 2 (JULY 2011), pp. 255-274; visit also https://www.ganintegrity.com/portal/country-profiles/zambia/

corruption. These acts have been criminalised under Part III of the Act which deems them as "corrupt practices". It has to be borne in mind that by section 3 of the Act, one is corrupt or engages in corruption if they participate in conduct amounting to "soliciting, accepting, obtaining, giving, promising or offering of a gratification by way of a bribe or other personal temptation or inducement, or the misuse or abuse of a public office for advantage or benefit for oneself or another person".

i.   *Corrupt practices by, or with, public officers*

Public officer means any person who is a member of, holds office in, is employed in the service of, or performs a function for or provides a public service for, a public body, whether such membership, office, service, function or employment is permanent or temporary, appointed or elected, full-time or part time, or paid or unpaid.[101] A public official means a person who performs a public function or provides a public service.[102] Public office means an office whose emoluments are paid directly from the consolidated fund or directly out of money provided and as approved by Parliament.[103] Section 19 of the AC Act creates an offence

---

[101] Section 3 of the AC Act

[102] Article 266 of the Constitution (Amendment) Act No. 2 of 2016 defines a public office as an office whose emoluments and expenses are a charge on the Consolidated Fund or other prescribed public fund and includes a State office, Constitutional office and an office in the public service, including that of a member of a commission; and a public officer as a person holding or acting in a public office, but does not include a State officer, councillor, a Constitutional office holder, a judge and a judicial officer.

[103] National Anti-Corruption Policy, 2009 at p.vii

when:

(1) A public officer who, by oneself, or by or in conjunction with, any other person, corruptly solicits, accepts or obtains, or agrees to accept or attempts to receive or obtain, from any person for oneself or for any other person, any gratification as an inducement or reward for doing or forbearing to do, or for having done or forborne to do, anything in relation to any matter or transaction, actual or proposed, with which any public body is or may be concerned, commits an offence.

(2) A person who, by oneself, or by, or in conjunction with, any other person, corruptly gives, promises or offers any gratification to any public officer, whether for the benefit of that public officer or of any other public officer, as an inducement or reward for doing or forbearing to do, anything in relation to any matter or transaction, actual or proposed, with which any public body is or may be concerned, commits an offence.

ii.   Corrupt transactions by, or with, private bodies

A private body, by section 3 of the AC Act, means a voluntary organisation, non-governmental organisation, political party, charitable institution, company, partnership, club or any other person or organisation which is not a public body. Section 20 of the AC Act has extended corruption to private bodies as it creates an offence involving transactions by or with private bodies. This provision states that:

> (1) A person who, by oneself, or by, or in conjunction with, any other person, corruptly solicits, accepts or obtains, or agrees to accept or attempts to receive or obtain, from any person for oneself or for any other person, any gratification as an inducement or reward for doing or forbearing to do, or for and having done or forborne to do, anything in relation to any matter or transaction actual or proposed, with which any private body is or may be concerned, commits an offence.

> (2) A person who, by oneself, or by, or in conjunction with, any other person, corruptly gives, promises or offers any gratification to any person, whether for the benefit of that person or of any other person, as an inducement or reward for doing or forbearing to do, or for having done or forborne to do, anything in relation to any matter or transaction, actual or proposed, with which any private body is or may be concerned,

commits an offence.[104]

iii.   *Corrupt transactions by, or with, agents*

An agent means a person employed by, or acting for, another and includes an officer of a public body or private body who acts for, or on behalf of, a public body or a private body or any other person, a trustee, an executor or an administrator of an estate of a deceased person.[105] By section 23 of the AC Act, agents are capable of indictment for corrupt practices where:

> (1) An agent who, with or without the principal's knowledge or concurrence, corruptly solicits, accepts or obtains, or agrees to accept or attempts to receive or obtain, from any person for oneself or for any other person, any gratification as an inducement or reward for doing or forbearing to do, or for having done or forborne to do, anything in relation to the principal's affairs or business, or for showing or having shown favour or

---

[104] Section 50 of the Act provides for the prosecution of directors and managers personally for offences committed by corporate or unincorporate bodies subject to certain exceptions. This provisions states that "Where an offence under this Act is committed by a body corporate or unincorporate body, every director or manager of the body corporate or unincorporate body shall be liable, upon conviction, as if the director or manager had personally committed the offence, unless the director or manager proves to the satisfaction of the court that the act constituting the offence was done without the knowledge, consent or connivance of the director or manager or that the director or manager took reasonable steps to prevent the commission of the offence."
[105] Section 3

disfavour to any person in relation to the principal's affairs or business, commits an offence.

(2) A person who corruptly gives, promises or offers any gratification to an agent as an inducement or reward for doing or forbearing to do, or for having done or forborne to do, anything in relation to the principal's affairs or business, or for showing or having shown favour or disfavour to any person in relation to the principal's affairs or business, commits an offence.

(3) A person who gives to an agent, or any agent who, with intent to deceive the principal, uses any receipt, account or other document in respect of which the principal is interested or which relates to the principal's affairs or business and which contains any statement which is false or erroneous or defective in any material particular, and which to the agent's knowledge or belief is intended to mislead the principal, commits an offence.

iv. *Corruption of members of public or private bodies with regard to meetings*

It is an offence for a person who being a member of any public or private body by oneself, or by, or in conjunction with, any other person, corruptly solicits, accepts or obtains, or agrees to accept or attempts to receive or obtain, from any person for oneself or for any other person, any gratification as an inducement or reward for—

(a) that person's voting or abstaining from voting at any meeting of such public or private body in favour of, or against, any measure, matter, resolution or question submitted to such public or private body;

(b) that person's performing or abstaining from performing, or for that person's aid in procuring, expediting, delaying, hindering or preventing the performance of, any official act by such public or private body; or

(c) that person's aid in procuring or preventing the passing of any vote or the granting of any contract or advantage in favour of any person; commits an offence.[106]

It is equally an offence for a person either, by oneself or in conjunction with, any other person, corruptly gives, promises or offers any gratification to a member of any public or private body in any circumstance referred to above.[107]

v. *Corruption of witnesses*

Any person who, directly or indirectly, corrupts a witness

---

[106] Section 24 (1)
[107] Section 24 (2)

so as to induce false testimony, an advantage or benefit for oneself or another person from the witness in a trial, hearing or other proceeding before any court, tribunal, judicial officer, committee, commission or any officer authorised by law to hear evidence or take testimony commits an offence and is liable, upon conviction, to imprisonment for a period not exceeding seven years.[108] In the same vein, any person who, by oneself, or by, or in conjunction with, any other person, corruptly promises, offers or gives any gratification to any witness whether for the benefit of that witness or any other person, with intent to influence the witness to be absent from trial, to give false testimony or withhold testimony, commits an offence and is liable, upon conviction, to imprisonment for a period not exceeding seven years.[109]

Equally, any witness who, by oneself or by, or in conjunction with, any other person, corruptly solicits, accepts or receives, or agrees to accept or attempts to receive or obtain, from any person for oneself or another person, any gratification as an inducement or reward whether for the witness's benefit or any other person, in order for the witness to be absent from trial or to give false testimony or withhold testimony, commits an offence and is liable, upon conviction, to imprisonment for a period not exceeding seven years.[110]

---

[108] Section 25 (1)
[109] Section 25 (2)
[110] Section 25 (3)

Related to this is the offence of obstruction of justice. Obstruction of justice is the interference with the orderly administration of law and justice, as by giving false information to or withholding evidence from a police officer or prosecutor, or by harming or intimidating a witness or juror.[111] This offence is provided under section 31 which states that:

> (1) A person who, by use of corrupt means or with intent to pervert the course of justice, interferes with the exercise of official duties by a judge, magistrate, judicial officer or any other arbiter or law enforcement officer, commits an offence and is liable, upon conviction, to imprisonment for a period not exceeding seven years.

> (2) A person who accepts or obtains, agrees to accept or attempts to obtain, or offers or gives, a gratification for oneself or for any other person in consideration of that person

> —

> (a) concealing an offence;

> (b) shielding any other person from legal proceedings for an offence;

> (c) not proceeding against any other person in

---

[111] B.A. Garner (ed.). (2009). Black's Law Dictionary, 9th edn., Minnesota: Thomson Reuters at p.1183

relation to an alleged offence; or (d) abandoning or withdrawing, or obtaining or endeavouring to obtain the withdrawal of, a prosecution against any other person;

commits an offence and is liable, upon conviction, to imprisonment for a period not exceeding seven years.

vi. Corrupt practices by, or with, foreign public official

In Zambia, corruption may be committed by a Zambian national acting in cahoots with a foreign public official and *vice versa*. The case of *Andrew Banda v The People*[112] is testament on how corrupt practices may occur between Zambian nationals or public officers with foreign officials or entities.[113] Section 26 of the AC Act provides that:

(1) A person who, by oneself or by, or in conjunction with, any other person, corruptly promises, offers or gives any gratification to any foreign public official, whether for the benefit of that foreign public official or any other person, as an inducement or reward for

---

[112] Appeal No. HPA/58/2014 (Unreported)

[113] Section 3 states that "foreign public official " means— (a) a person holding any executive, legislative, administrative or judicial office at any level of the government of a foreign State; (b) any person performing public functions for a foreign State, or any board, commission, corporation or other body or authority performing a duty or function on behalf of the foreign State; or (c) an official or agent of a public international organisation formed by two or more States or two or more public international organisations; and "foreign state" as any country other than Zambia.

doing or forbearing to do, or for having done or forborne to do, anything in relation to any matter or transaction, actual or proposed, with which any foreign public body is or may be concerned, commits an offence.

(2) A foreign public official who, by oneself or by, or in conjunction with, any other person corruptly solicits, accepts or obtains, or agrees to accept or attempts to receive or obtain, from any person for oneself or for any other person, any gratification as an inducement or reward for doing or forbearing to do, or for having done or forborne to do, anything in relation to any matter or transaction, actual or proposed, with which any foreign public body is or may be concerned, commits an offence.

(3) A person who unlawfully promises, offers, or gives to a foreign public official, directly or indirectly, an undue advantage, for the benefit of the foreign public official or another person, in order that the public official may do or forbear to do, in the exercise of the official duties, in order to obtain or retain business or other undue advantage in relation to the conduct of international affairs or business, commits an offence.

(4) A foreign public official who solicits or accepts, directly or indirectly, an undue

advantage, for the benefit of the foreign public official or another person, in order that the foreign public official may act or refrain from acting in the exercise of official duties, commits an offence.

vii.   Corruption in relation to sporting events

Corruption in the sporting world has become a bigger vice that imagined. The blow-up at the *Fédération Internationale de Football Association* (FIFA) that led to widespread indictments of top football officials globally has made corruption in sport a bigger problem. Section 27 of the AC Act creates corruption offences related to sporting events. This provision states that:

A person who, directly or indirectly, corruptly —

(a) solicits or accepts or agrees to accept any gratification, whether for the benefit of that person or any other person, as an inducement or reward for a person influencing or having influenced the run of play or the outcome of any sporting event; or

(b) offers or gives or agrees to give to any other person any gratification as an inducement to influence or as a reward for influencing or having influenced the run of play or the outcome of a sporting event;

commits an offence.

viii. Corrupt acquisition of public property and revenue

Public property means property belonging to or under the control of, or consigned or due to, a public body.[114] It is an offence for one to engage in corrupt practices in the acquisition of public property and revenue. Section 34 of the AC Act provides that:

(1) A person who, by oneself or with or through another person, fraudulently or unlawfully —

(a) acquires public funds or property or a public service or benefit for that person's or another person's benefit;

(b) diverts any public property for purposes other than for what it is intended, for that person's or another person's benefit;

(c) mortgages, charges or disposes of any public property for that person's or another person's benefit; or

(d) obtains any exemption, remission, reduction or abatement from payment of any tax, fee, levy or charge required to be paid under any law; commits an offence.

---

[114] Section 3

(2) A person whose functions concern the administration, custody, management, receipt or use of any public revenue or public property or in whom any public revenue or public property is vested by virtue of that person's position or office, commits an offence if that person —

(a) fraudulently facilitates or makes payment from the public revenue for —

(i) sub-standard or defective goods;

(ii) goods not supplied or not supplied in full; or

(iii) services not rendered or not adequately rendered; or

(b) wilfully fails to comply with any law or applicable procedure or guideline relating to the procurement, allocation, sale or disposal of property, tendering of contracts, management of funds or incurring of public expenditure.

(3) A person who administers, keeps, manages, receives or uses any private funds or property, who fraudulently or unlawfully —

(a) acquires private funds or property for that person's or another person's benefit; or

(b) misappropriates the private funds or property; commits an offence.

ix.   *Electoral corruption*

Electoral corruption means any illicit activity committed under the electoral laws and regulations from which a benefit or advantage is realised or derived, directly or indirectly.[115] Electoral corruption is sometimes termed political corruption or electoral malpractices and is criminalised in this jurisdiction not only by the AC Act but also by the Electoral Process Act.[116] Section 35 (2) of the AC provides that it is an offence for a person use any funds acquired through illegal or corrupt practices to fund a political party or for any purpose related to an election.

However, Part VIII of the Electoral Process Act provides a comprehensive list of offences related to corruption, bribery and undue influence:

> 81. (1) A person shall not, either directly or indirectly, by oneself or with any other person corruptly—
>
> (a) give, lend, procure, offer, promise or agree to give, lend, procure or offer, any money to a voter or to any other person on behalf of a voter or for the benefit of a voter in order to induce that voter to vote or refrain from

---

[115] National Anti-Corruption Policy, 2009 at p. vi
[116] No. 35 of 2016

voting or corruptly do any such act as aforesaid on account of such voter having voted or refrained from voting at any election;

(b) give, lend or procure, offer, promise or agree to give, lend, procure, offer or promise, any money to a voter or for the benefit of a voter or to any other person or on behalf of that person on behalf of any voter or to or for any other person for acting or joining in any procession or demonstration before, during or after any election;

(c) make any gift, loan, offer, promise, procurement or agreement to or for the benefit of any person in order to induce the person to procure or to endeavour to procure the return of any candidate at any election or the vote of any voter at any election;

(d) upon or in consequence of any gift, loan, offer, promise, procurement or agreement, procure or engage, promise or endeavour to procure, the return of any candidate at any election or the vote of any voter at any election;

(e) advance or pay or cause to be advanced or paid any money to or for the use of any other person with the intent that such money or any part thereof shall be expended in bribery at any election, or knowingly pay or cause to be paid any money to any person in discharge or repayment of any money wholly or partially expended in bribery at any election;

(f)before or during any election, receive or contract for any money or loan for oneself or for any other person for voting or agreeing to vote or for refraining or agreeing to refrain from voting at any election;

(g) after any election, receive any money on account of any person having voted or refrained from voting or having induced any other person to vote or refrain from voting at any election; or

(h) convey or transfer or be concerned with the conveyance or transfer of any property, or pay or be concerned with the payment of any money, to any person for the purpose of enabling that person to be registered as a voter, thereby to influence that person's vote at any future election, or pay to or be concerned with the payment of any money on account of any voter for the purpose of inducing that person to vote or refrain from voting.

(2) A person who contravenes any provision of subsection (1) commits an offence.

(3) Nothing in this Act shall be construed as applying to any money paid or agreed to be paid for, or on account of, any expenditure bona fide and lawfully incurred in respect of the conduct or management of an election.

83. (1) A person shall not directly or indirectly, by oneself or through any other person—

(a) make use of or threaten to make use of any force, violence or restraint upon any other person;

(b) inflict or threaten to inflict by oneself or by any other person, or by any supernatural or non-natural means, or pretended supernatural or non-natural means, any physical, psychological, mental or spiritual injury, damage, harm or loss upon or against any person;

(c) do or threaten to do anything to the disadvantage of any person in order to induce or compel any person—

(i) to register or not to register as a voter;

(ii) to vote or not to vote;

(iii) to vote or not to vote for any registered political party or candidate;

(iv) to support or not to support any political registered party or candidate; or

(v) to attend and participate in, or not to attend and participate in, any political meeting, march, demonstration or other political event;

(d) interfere with the independence or impartiality of the Commission, any member, employee or officer of the Commission;

(e) prejudice any person because of any past, present or anticipated performance of a function under this Act;

(f) advantage, or promise to advantage, a person in exchange for that person not performing a function under this Act; or

(g) unlawfully prevent the holding of any political meeting, march, demonstration or other political event.

(2) Subject to the other provisions of this Act, a person shall not prevent another person from exercising a right conferred by this Act.

(3) A person, knowing that another person is not entitled to be registered as a voter, shall not—

(a) persuade that other person that, that other

person is entitled to be registered as a voter; or

(b) represent to anyone else that the person is entitled to be registered as a voter.

(4) A person, knowing that another person is not entitled to vote shall not—

(a) assist, compel or persuade that other person to vote; or (b) represent to anyone else that the other person is entitled to vote.

(5) A person who contravenes any of the provisions of subsections (1) to (4) commits an offence.

(6) A person who, by abduction, duress or any fraudulent device or contrivance, impedes or prevents the free exercise of the vote of any voter or thereby compels, induces or prevails upon any voter either to give or to refrain from giving the person's vote at any election, commits an offence.[117]

---

[117] See Chapter 2 in Majula, R.R. (2008). The Impact of Corruption on Public Administration in Zambia. Lusaka: Zambia Educational Publishing House for a detailed study on political corruption and its effects on public administration; see also Reuben Mtolo Phiri (Male) v Lameck Mangani (Male), SCZ Judgment No. 2 of 2013

x.   Conflict of interest

A conflict of interest arises where there is a real or seeming incompatibility between one's private interests and one's public or fiduciary duties.[118] A person commits an offence when they fail to adhere to the provisions of section 28 (1) and (2) of the AC Act which state that:

> (1) Where a public body in which a public officer is a member, director, employee or is otherwise engaged proposes to deal with any person or company, partnership or other undertaking in which that public officer has a direct or indirect private or personal interest, that public officer shall forthwith disclose, in writing to that public body, the nature of such interest and shall not take part in any proceedings or process of that public body relating to such decision.

> (2) Where a public officer or a relative or associate of such public officer has a personal interest in a decision to be taken by a public body, that public officer shall forthwith disclose, in writing to that public body, the nature of such interest and shall not vote or take part in any proceedings or process of that public body relating to such decision.

---

[118] Black's Law Dictionary at p.341

4.2 Bribery

A bribe means a gift of money, favour or material given to persuade someone to do or not to do something.[119] Bribery on the other hand means the act of offering someone money or other valuables, in order to persuade him or her to do or not to do something.[120] It is the receiving or offering of any undue reward by or to any person whatsoever, in a public office, in order to influence his or her behaviour in office, and incline him or her to act contrary to the known rules of honesty and integrity.[121] It is an offence of bribery not only to give or receive a bribe, but also to offer or solicit a bribe.[122] Offering and receiving are unilateral acts and do not depend on any state of mind on the part of the person offering the bribe or the person solicited.[123]

4.3 Abuse of office

The offence of abuse of authority of office is committed by public officers when they do any of the acts outlined under section 21 of the AC Act. For avoidance of doubt, a public officer is any person who is a member of, holds office in, is employed in the service of, or performs a function for or provides a public service for, a public body, whether such membership, office, service, function or employment is

---

[119] National Anti-Corruption Policy, 2009 at p.v
[120] id
[121] David Lanham, 'Bribery and Corruption,' in P. Smith (ed.) (1987). Criminal Law: Essays in Honor of J.C. Smith. London: Butterworths at pp.92-93
[122] Corruption and misuse of public office, 2nd edn. At p.21
[123] id

permanent or temporary, appointed or elected, full-time or part time, or paid or unpaid.[124] The position of the law, as outlined in the aforesaid section, is that:

(1) A public officer commits an offence who —

(a) does, or directs to be done, in abuse of the public officer's position, office or authority any arbitrary act prejudicial to the rights or interests of the Government or any other person;

(b) uses that public officer's position, office or authority or any information that the public officer obtains as a result of, or in the course of, the performance of that public officer's functions to obtain property, profit, an advantage or benefit, directly or indirectly, for oneself or another person;

(c) uses the public officer's position, office or information to obtain, promise, offer, or give an undue advantage to oneself or another person, directly or indirectly, in order for the public officer to perform or refrain from performing the public officer's duties; or

(d) solicits or accepts directly or indirectly an undue advantage or benefit for oneself or for

---

[124] Section 3 of the AC Act

another person in order for the public officer to perform or refrain from performing the public officer's duties.

(2) For the purposes of subsection (1), a public officer shall be presumed, until the contrary is proved, to have used that public officer's position, office or information for an advantage or benefit where the public officer takes any decision or action in relation to any matter in which the public officer or a relative or associate of that public officer, has a direct or indirect interest.

(3) A public officer who, being concerned with any matter or transaction falling within, or connected with, that public officer's jurisdiction, powers, duties or functions, corruptly solicits, accepts or obtains, or agrees to accept or attempts to receive or obtain for oneself or for any other person any gratification in relation to such matter or transaction, commits an offence.

(4) A person who, being concerned with any matter or transaction falling within the scope of authority, or connected with the jurisdiction, powers, duties or functions of any public officer, by oneself, or by, or in conjunction with, any other person, corruptly gives, promises or offers any gratification,

whether directly or indirectly, to such public officer either for oneself or for any other person, commits an offence.

(5) A public officer who unreasonably delays, refuses, neglects or omits to perform that public officer's duties or functions in order to procure or induce a person to offer or give gratification to that public officer, commits an offence.[125]

4.4 Solicitation and Gratification

Solicitation is not defined under statute in Zambia but we can borrow from the American case of *State v Wallace*[126] which defined the term to mean asking, enticing, or requesting of another to commit a crime of bribery. It was further stated that to constitute the crime of solicitation of a bribe, it is not necessary that the act be actually consummated or that the defendant profit by it as it is sufficient if a bribe was actually solicited.

Gratification means any corrupt payment, whether in cash or kind, any rebate, bonus, deduction or material gain, benefit, amenity, facility, advantage or gift, or any other thing obtained as a result of the corrupt misuse or abuse of public funds or property, other than a casual gift.[127] By

---

[125] See the cases of Lt. Gen. Geojago Robert Chaswe Musengule and Amon Sibande v The People, HPA /16/2009; The People v Zeles Kunja Zulu and Top Motors Limited, 2SPC/123/12;

[126] 214 A.2d 886, 889 (Del. Super. Ct. 1963)

[127] National Anti-Corruption Policy, 2009 at p.vi

section 3 of the AC Act, gratification includes:

(a) money, any gift, loan, fee, reward, commission, valuable security, property, or interest in property of any description, whether movable or immovable;

(b) any employment or contract of employment or services and any promise to give employment or render services in any capacity;

(c) any payment, release, discharge or liquidation of any loan, obligation or other liability, whether in whole or in part;

(d) any service, favour or advantage of any description, such as protection from any penalty or from any action or proceedings of a disciplinary or penal nature, and including the exercise or the omission from the exercise of any right of any official power or duty;

(e) any valuable consideration or benefit of any kind, discount, commission, rebate, bonus deduction or percentage;

(f) any right or privilege; and

(g) any aid, vote, consent or influence.

The case of *The People v Davy Siame*[128] conceptualises the offences of solicitation and gratification. In this case, the accused person stood charged with one count of corrupt practices contrary to section 19 (1) of the AC Act No. 3 of 2012. The particulars alleged that the accused on dates unknown but between 1st August, 2014 and 30th September, 2015 at Lusaka in the Lusaka District of the Lusaka Province of the Republic of Zambia, being a public officer, namely a Legal Assistant in the Prosecutions Section of the Legal Department at Lusaka City Council, corruptly solicited and actually received ZMW 3000.00 cash gratification from Brian Mwiinga as an inducement or reward in order for him to assist the said Brian Mwiinga secure the release of a motor vehicle registration number ALK 4012 which was impounded by the Road Transport and Safety Agency (RTSA), a public body. The court guided that for the charge to stand, the prosecution must prove the following:

i. The accused person being a public officer;

ii. Corruptly solicited, and;

iii. Actually received cash money from one Brian Mwiinga;

iv. Being gratification as an inducement or reward to assist the said person secure the release of an impounded motor vehicle;

v. From a public body.

---

[128] IPG/180/2015

Gratification for giving assistance, etc. with regard to contracts

The case of *Lieutenant General Geojago Robert Chaswe Musengule and Amon Sibande v The People*[129] illustrates the nature of this offence. In this case, the brief facts are that the accused person, who served as Zambia Air Force (ZAF) Commander, was alleged to have solicited and received gratification from Base Chemicals Limited as a reward for awarding a contract for the supply of equipment and materials to ZAF. Section 29 of the AC Act proscribes such acts and conduct. The said provision states that:

> (1) A public officer who, directly or indirectly, by oneself, or by, or in conjunction with, any other person, corruptly solicits, accepts or obtains, or agrees to accept or attempts to receive or obtain, from any person for oneself or for any other person, any gratification as an inducement or reward for or otherwise on account of, that public officer giving assistance or using influence in, or having given assistance or used influence in—
>
> (a) the promotion, execution or procurement of—
>
> (i) any contract with a public body or private body for the performance of any work, the provision of any service, the doing of anything or the supplying of any article,

---

[129] supra

material or substance; or

(ii) any sub-contract to perform any work, provide any service, do anything or supply any article, material or substance required to be performed, provided, done or supplied under any contract with a public body or private body; or

(b) the payment of the price, consideration or other moneys stipulated or otherwise provided for in any contract or sub-contract; commits an offence.

(2) A person who corruptly gives, promises or offers any gratification to any public officer as an inducement or reward for, or otherwise on account of, such public officer giving assistance or using influence in, or having given assistance or used influence in—

(a) the promotion, execution or procurement of; or

(b) the payment of the price, consideration or other moneys stipulated or otherwise provided for in; any contract or sub-contract commits an offence.

Gratification for procuring withdrawal of tender

It is an offence for any person who, directly or indirectly, by oneself, or by, or in conjunction with, any other person, corruptly solicits, accepts or obtains, or agrees to accept or attempts to receive or obtain from any person for oneself or for any other person, any gratification as an inducement or reward for, or otherwise on account of, the withdrawal of a tender, or the refraining from the making of a tender for any contract with a public body or private body for the performance of any work, the provision of any service, the doing of anything or the supplying of any article, material or substance.[130] It also an offence for a person to corruptly give, promise or offer any gratification to any other person as an inducement or reward for, or otherwise on account of, the withdrawal of a tender, or the refraining from making of a tender for a contract.[131]

Gratification with regard to bidding at auction sale

Any person who, directly or indirectly by oneself, or by, or in conjunction with, any other person, corruptly solicits, accepts or obtains, or agrees to accept or attempts to receive or obtain, from any person for oneself or for any other person, any gratification as an inducement or reward for, or otherwise on account of, that person refraining or having refrained from bidding at any sale by auction conducted by, or on behalf of, any public body or private body, commits an offence under section 30 of the AC Act. It is equally an offence under the same section if a person corruptly gives, promises or offers any gratification to any

---

[130] Section 30 (1)
[131] Section 30 (2)

other person as an inducement or reward for, or otherwise on account of, that other person's refraining or having refrained from bidding at an auction.

Dealing with, using and concealing gratification

This offence is created by section 37 of the AC Act. This provision states that:

(1) A person who, directly or indirectly, whether on that person's behalf or any other person, knowingly —

(a) enters into, or causes to be entered into, any dealing in relation to any proceeds of crime; or

(b) uses or causes to be used, or receives, holds, controls or conceals any property or any part thereof, which was obtained as gratification, or derived from the proceeds of crime obtained in the commission of an offence under this Part; commits an offence.

(2) For purposes of subsection (1), "dealing" includes —

(a) any purchase, sale, loan, charge, mortgage, lien, pledge, transfer, delivery, assignment, subrogation, transmission, gift, trust, settlement, deposit, withdrawal, transfer between accounts or extension of credit;

(b) any agency or grant of power of attorney; or

(c) any act which results in any right, interest, title or privilege, whether present or future or whether vested or contingent, in the whole or in part of any property being conferred on any person.[132]

4.5 Possession of unexplained property

Unexplained property means property in respect of which the value is disproportionate to a person's known sources of income at or around the time of the commission of the

---

[132] It must be noted as well that concealment of any offence under Part III of the AC Act is proscribed. Section 38 of the Act provides that:
A person commits an offence who, with intent to defraud or to conceal the commission of an offence under this Part, or to obstruct an officer in the investigation of any offence — (a) destroys, alters, mutilates or falsifies any book, document, valuable security, account, computer system, disk, computer printout or other electronic device which belongs to, or is in the possession of, or has been received by that person or that person's employer, or any entry in such book, document, account or electronic device, or is privy to any such act; (b) makes or is privy to the making of any false entry in any book, document, account or electronic device; or (c) omits or is privy to the omission of any information from any book, document, account or electronic device. A duty has also been placed on public officers to report gratification to relevant authorities failure to which that officer may be charged under section 39 which provides that:
(1) A public officer to whom any gratification is corruptly given, promised or offered shall make a full report of the circumstances of the case to an officer of the Commission or a police officer within twenty-four hours of the occurrence of the event, and if the public officer fails to do so without reasonable cause, the public officer commits an offence and is liable, upon conviction, to a fine not exceeding two hundred thousand penalty units or to imprisonment for a period not exceeding two years, or to both. (2) An officer of the Commission or a police officer may arrest without warrant any person in respect of whom a report is made under subsection (1).

offence and for which there is no satisfactory explanation.[133] Section 22 of the Act provides for this offence which states that:

> (1) Subject to the Constitution, any public officer who -

> (a) maintains a standard of living above which is commensurate with the public officer's present or past official emoluments or other income;

> (b) is in control or possession of pecuniary resources or property disproportionate to the public officer's present or past official emoluments; or

> (c) is in receipt of the benefit of any services which the public officer may reasonably be suspected of having received corruptly or in circumstances which amount to an offence under this Act;

> shall, unless the contrary is proved, be liable for the offence of having, or having had under the public officer's control or in the public officer's possession pecuniary resources or property reasonably suspected of having been corruptly acquired, or having misused or abused the public officer's office,

---

[133] Section 3 of the AC Act

as the case may be.

(2) Where a court is satisfied in proceedings for an offence under subsection (1) that, having regard to the closeness of the public officer's relationship to the accused and to other relevant circumstances, there is reason to believe that any person was holding pecuniary resources or property in trust for or otherwise on behalf of the accused, or acquired such pecuniary resources or property as a gift, or loan without adequate consideration, from the accused, such pecuniary resources or property shall, unless the contrary is proved, be deemed to have been under the control or in the possession of the accused.

The ACC may commence proceedings for forfeiture of unexplained property under this section against a person where — (a) after due investigation, the Commission is satisfied that the person has unexplained assets; and (b) the person has, in the course of the exercise by the Commission of its powers of investigation or otherwise, been afforded a reasonable opportunity to explain the disproportion between the assets concerned and the person's known legitimate sources of income and the Commission is not satisfied that an adequate explanation of that disproportion has been given.[134]

4.6 Concealment of property

Property includes any real or personal property, money, things in action or other intangible or incorporeal property, whether located in Zambia or elsewhere, and property of corresponding value in the absence of the original illegally acquired property whose value has been determined.[135] It an offence under section 36 of the AC Act for one to conceal property which is suspected to be proceeds of corruption.

The case of *The People v Austin Chisangu Liato*[136] is a classic case on the operation of this offence in relation to concealment of property. In this case, the respondent was arraigned, tried and convicted by the Subordinate Court of the First Class on one count of possession of property suspected of being proceeds of crime contrary to section 71 (1) of the Forfeiture of Proceeds of Crime Act No. 19 of 20101, of the laws of Zambia. The particulars of the offence were that the respondent, on the 24th November, 2011 at Lusaka in the Lusaka District of the Lusaka Province of the Republic of Zambia, did possess and conceal money at his farm, namely No. L/Mpamba/44, Mwembeshi, amounting to K2, 100,100,000, being reasonably suspected of being proceeds of crime. After hearing six prosecution witnesses, and the respondent

---

[134] Section 62

[135] Section 3

[136] Appeal No. 291/2014

having opted to remain silent, the learned trial Magistrate, in a judgment delivered on 23rd July, 2013, was satisfied that, on the totality of the evidence before her, the prosecution had proved the case against the respondent to the requisite standard. She convicted the respondent and subsequently sentenced him to twenty-four months imprisonment with hard labour. She also ordered forfeiture of the K2, 100,100,000 and the farm to the State.

The said section 36 of the AC Act provides as follows:

A person who —

(a) converts, transfers or disposes of property, knowing that such property is the proceeds of corruption or related offences for the purpose of concealing or disguising the illicit origin of the property or of helping any other person who is involved in the commission of the offence to evade the consequences of that person's action;

(b) conceals or disguises the true nature, source, location, disposition, movement or ownership of, or rights with respect to, property which is from the proceeds of corruption or related offences; or

(c) acquires, possesses or uses any property with the knowledge at the time of receipt, that such property is from the proceeds of corruption or related offences;

commits an offence and is liable, upon conviction, to imprisonment for a period not exceeding two years.

4.7 Attempts and conspiracies

Conceptualising attempts and conspiracy in criminal law

When criminal law talks of attempts and conspiracies it speaks of preparatory or inchoate offences. This means offences that have just began but cannot materialise or brought to a finality owing to different reasons, including impossibility of effecting the criminal act due to ignorance or inability among others.[137] An attempt is an overt act that is done with the intent to commit a crime but that falls short of completing the crime.[138] Section 389 of the Penal Code Act, Chapter 87 of the laws of Zambia defines attempts when it provides that:

(1) When a person, intending to commit an offence, begins to put his intention into execution by means adapted to its fulfilment, and manifests his intention by some overt act, but does not fulfil his intention to such an

---

[137] See Chapter 10 of Kulusika, S.E. (2020). Criminal Law in Zambia: Doctrine Theory and Practice. Lusaka: Chribwa Publsihers; and Chapter 6 of Hatchard, J. and Ndulo, M. (2008). A Case Book on Criminal Law. Lusaka: Institute for Public Policy Research

[138] Black's Law Dictionary at p.146

extent as to commit the offence, he is deemed
to attempt to commit the offence.

(2) It is immaterial, except so far as regards
punishment, whether the offender does all
that is necessary on his part for completing
the commission of the offence, or whether
the complete fulfilment of his intention is
prevented by circumstances independent of
his will, or whether he desists of his own
motion from the further prosecution of his
intention.

(3) It is immaterial that by reason of
circumstances not known to the offender it is
impossible in fact to commit the offence.

On the other hand, a conspiracy is an agreement by two or
more persons to commit an unlawful act, coupled with an
intent to achieve the agreement's objective, and an action
or conduct that furthers the agreement.[139] The essential
aspects of conspiracy include an agreement to commit an
offence, or to commit lawful acts by unlawful means, and
there must be two or more persons to the conspiracy.[140]
The generally accepted and authoritative definition of the
offence under common law was posited by Willes, J. in the
celebrated case of *Mulcahy v R*[141] when he opined that:

---

[139] Black's Law Dictionary at p.351
[140] Criminal Law in Zambia: Doctrine Theory and Practice at p. 385
[141] (1868), 3 HL at p.317

A conspiracy consists not merely in the intention of two or more but in the agreement of two or more to do an unlawful act, or to do a lawful act by unlawful means. So long as a design rests in the intention only it is not indictable. When two agree to carry it into effect, the very plot is an act in itself, and the act of each the parties…punishable if for a criminal object or for the use of criminal means.

The gist of the offence of conspiracy lies, as Foster-Sutton, P. reasoned in the case of *Majekodunmi v The Queen*,[142] not in doing the act, or effecting the purpose for which the conspiracy is formed, but in the forming of the scheme or agreement between the parties. Sections 394 to 397 of the Penal Code contains definitions of conspiracy in the following terms:

394. Any person who conspires with another to commit any felony, or to do any act in any part of the world which if done in Zambia would be a felony, and which is an offence under the laws in force in the place where it is proposed to be done, is guilty of a felony and is liable, if no other punishment is provided, to imprisonment for seven years, or, if the greatest punishment to which a person convicted of the felony in question is liable is less than imprisonment for seven years, then to such lesser punishment.

---

[142] (1952) 14 W.A.C.A. 64

395. Any person who conspires with another to commit a misdemeanour, or to do any act in any part of the world which if done in Zambia would be a misdemeanour, and which is an offence under the laws in force in the place where it is proposed to be done, is guilty of a misdemeanour.

396. Any person who conspires with another to effect any of the purposes following, that is to say:

(a) to prevent or defeat the execution or enforcement of any Act, Statute, or Order; or

(b) to cause any injury to the person or reputation of any person, or to depreciate the value of any property of any person; or

(c) to prevent or obstruct the free and lawful disposition of any property by the owner thereof for its fair value; or

(d) to injure any person in his trade or profession; or

(e) to prevent or obstruct, by means of any act or acts which if done by an individual person would constitute an offence on his part, the free and lawful exercise by any person of his trade, profession, or occupation; or

(f) to effect any unlawful purpose; or (g) to effect any lawful purpose by any unlawful means; is guilty of a misdemeanour:

Provided that an agreement or combination by two or more persons to do or procure to be done any act in contemplation or furtherance of a trade dispute, as defined in the Industrial and Labour Relations Act, shall not be punishable under the provisions of this section if such act committed by one person would not be punishable as a crime.

Attempts and conspiracy under the AC Act

Section 40 of the AC Act provides for attempts and conspiracies related to corruption related offences and corrupt practices. By this section, it is an offence for a person to aid, abet or counsel or conspire with any person to commit an offence under Part III of the AC Act and that person is liable, upon conviction, to a sentence as if that person committed the offence.[143] It is also an offence for a person to attempt to commit an offence under the AC Act and that person is liable, upon conviction, to a sentence as if that person committed the offence.[144]

---

[143] Subsection 1
[144] Subsection 2

4.8 Conclusion

This chapter has discussed mainly Part III of the AC Act by traversing offences termed corrupt practices under that Act. It has discussed the law as it relates to corruption and related offences by looking at not only the statutory position but in some cases the position at common law as well as under international instruments such as the AU Convention and the SADC Protocol.

CHAPTER

5

MONEY LAUNDERING AND RELATED OFFENCES

5.0 Introduction

This chapter will discuss primarily the offences of money laundering, terrorism financing and related offences. Money laundering (ML) and terrorism financing (TF) have become the most devastating form of economic crimes on most economies of the world. It is for this reason that the fight against these two and related crimes in the form of anti-money laundering - combating the financing of terrorism (AML/CFT) has been replicated from the global to regional and finally to national levels.

5.1 Conceptual Framework

Money laundering

The layperson's view of money laundering is that it is simply the 'cleaning of dirty money', that is, converting money obtained through criminal activities into clean money. Another narrow view is that it is simply the hiding of one's source of wealth gained through illegal activities such as corruption and bribery, drug trafficking, illegal arms sales, smuggling, embezzlement, insider dealing and trading and fraud among others.[145]However, it must be noted that money laundering encompasses a far wide range of criminal activities and is an attempt to hide the proceeds of crime (by integrating such proceeds into other legitimate property or by confusing the audit trail) in such a way that the authorities cannot trace the proceeds back to the original crime.[146]

The Financial Action Task Force (FATF), an intergovernmental organisation founded in 1989 on the initiative of the G7[147] to develop policies to combat money laundering, observes in trying to put the concept of money laundering into perspective that:

> The goal of a large number of criminal acts is to generate a profit for the individual or group that carries out the act. Money laundering is the processing of these criminal proceeds to disguise their illegal origin. This process is of critical importance, as it enables the criminal to enjoy these profits without jeopardizing their source.
>
> Illegal arms sales, smuggling, and the activities of organized crime, including for example

[145] See Olamide, O. (2019). Guide to Anti-Money Laundering in Nigeria. Middletown: Independent Publication at p.3

[146] Camp, P. (2009). Solicitors and Money Laundering: A Compliance Handbook. London: Law Society at p.4

[147] The Group of Seven (G7) is an intergovernmental organization consisting of Canada, France, Germany, Italy, Japan, the United Kingdom and the United States.

drug trafficking and prostitution rings, can generate huge amounts of proceeds. Embezzlement, insider trading, bribery and computer fraud schemes can also produce large profits and create the incentive to "legitimize" the ill-gotten gains through money laundering.

When a criminal activity generates substantial profits, the individual or group involved must find a way to control the funds without attracting attention to the underlying activity or the persons involved. Criminals do this by disguising the sources, changing the form, or moving the funds to a place where they are less likely to attract attention.

Money laundering under statute

The Prohibition and Prevention of Money Laundering Act of 2001 (PPMLA) is the leading legislation regarding the combating of money laundering in Zambia. Section 2 of the Act defines the term money laundering to mean: first, engaging, directly or indirectly, in a business trans- action that involves property acquired with proceeds of crime; second, receiving, possessing, concealing, disguising, disposing of or bringing into Zambia, any property derived or realised directly or indirectly from illegal activity; or third, the retention or acquisition of property knowing that the property is, derived or realised, directly or indirectly, from illegal activity.

Terrorism and proliferation financing

Terrorism and proliferation financing are regulated by the Anti-Terrorism and Non-Proliferation Act of 2018. As a foundation for this discourse, it is imperative to understand the meaning of terrorism and proliferation under Zambian law. Section 3 of the Anti-Terrorism Act defines these concepts in detail in the following ways:

Terrorism

Terrorism means an act or omission in or outside Zambia that is intended, or by its nature and context, may reasonably be regarded as being intended to intimidate or threaten the public or a section of the public or compel a government or an international organisation to do, or refrain from doing, any act, and is made for the purpose of advancing a political, ideological or religious cause and which —

(a) constitutes an offence within the scope of a counterterrorism convention listed in the Second Schedule;

(b) causes or is intended to cause death or serious bodily harm to a person;

(c) causes or is intended to cause serious damage to private or public property; (d) endangers a person's life;

(e) creates a serious risk to the health or safety

of the public or a section of the public;

(f) involves the use of firearms or explosives;

g) involves the release into the environment or any part thereof or distributing or exposing the public or any part thereof to any dangerous, hazardous, radioactive, harmful substance, toxic chemical, microbial or other biological agent or toxin;

(h) is designed or intended to disrupt any computer system or the provision of services directly related to communications, infrastructure, banking or financial services, utilities, transportation or other essential infrastructure or services;

(i) is designed or intended to disrupt the provision of essential emergency services such as police, civil defence or medical services;

(j) causes serious risk to national security;

(k) causes damage to a vessel or is likely to endanger the safe navigation of any vessel on inland or international waters; and

(l) causes damage to any aircraft or airport, is intended or likely to cause damage to any air navigation facilities or endanger the safety and lives of persons and property, affect the operations of air services or undermine the confidence of the public in the safety of civil aviation.[148]

Terrorism financing

Terrorism financing means an act by any person who, irrespective of whether a terrorist act occurs, by any means, directly or indirectly, wilfully provides or collects funds or attempts to do so with the intention that the funds should be used or knowing that the funds are to be used in full or in part—

(i)   to carry out a terrorist act;

(ii) by a terrorist;

(iii) by a terrorist organisation; or

(iv) for the travel of a person to a State other than the person's State of residence or nationality for the purpose of perpetration, planning or preparation of, or participation in, terrorist act or the providing or receiving of terrorist training.

---

[148] Section 3 states that "terrorist organisation " means a group of terrorists that— (a) commits, or attempts to commit, terrorist acts by any means, directly or indirectly, unlawfully and wilfully; (b) participates as an accomplice in terrorist acts; (c) organises or directs others to commit terrorist acts; or (d) contributes to the commission of terrorist acts by a group of persons acting with a common purpose where the contribution is made intentionally and with the aim of furthering the terrorist act or with the knowledge of the intention of the group to commit a terrorist act; and "terrorist" means a person who— (a) has committed an offence under this Act; or (b) is or has been involved in the commission, preparation or instigation of acts of terrorism.

Proliferation

Proliferation includes the manufacture, acquisition, possession, development, export, transhipment, brokering, transport, transfer, stockpiling, supply, sale or use of nuclear, ballistic, chemical, radiological or biological weapons or any other weapon capable of causing mass destruction and their means, of delivery and related materials, including both technologies and dual use goods used for non-legitimate purposes, including technology, goods, software, services or expertise, in contravention of this Act or, where applicable, international obligations derived from relevant Security Council Resolutions and "proliferation activity" shall be construed accordingly.[149]

Proliferation financing

Proliferation financing means an act by any person who by any means, directly or indirectly, wilfully or negligently provides funds or financial services to be used or knowing that they are to be used in whole or in part for proliferation, the manufacture, acquisition, possession, development, export, transhipment, brokering, transport, transfer, stockpiling, supply, sale or use of nuclear, ballistic, chemical, radiological or biological weapons or any other weapon capable of causing mass destruction and their means of delivery and related materials including both technologies and dual-use goods used for non-legitimate purposes, including technology, goods, software, services

---

[149] Section 3 states that "proliferation related entity" means an entity concerned with the facilitation of proliferation and proliferation financing.

or expertise, in contravention of this Act or, where applicable, international obligations derived from relevant Security Council Resolutions.

5.2 AML/CFT Legislation: International[150]

United Nations (UN) instruments/conventions

i. Vienna Convention: UN Convention Against Illicit Traffic in Narcotic Drugs and Psychotropic Substances of 1988 and its status;
ii. Palermo Convention: UN Convention Against Transnational Organized Crime of 2001 and its status;
iii. Merida Convention: UN Convention Against Corruption of 2005 and its status.
iv. International Convention for the Suppression of the Financing of Terrorism of 1999;
v. UN Security Council Resolutions.

FATF

i. Forty Recommendations on Money Laundering;
ii. Interpretative Notes to the Forty Recommendations;
iii. Methodology for Assessing Compliance with the FATF 40+9 Recommendations;
iv. Nine Special Recommendations on Terrorist Financing;

---

[150] Adapted from
https://www.imf.org/external/np/leg/amlcft/eng/aml4.htm#antimoney

v. Interpretative Note to Special Recommendations on Terrorist Financing;

vi. International Best Practices; and

vii. Methodology for Assessing Compliance with the FATF 40+9 Recommendations.

Model laws

a) Anti-Money Laundering

i. IMF/UNODC Model Legislation on money laundering and financing of terrorism (2005);

ii. UN ODCCP Model Legislation on Laundering, Confiscation and International Cooperation with regard to Illicit Traffic in Narcotic Drugs, Psychotropic Substances and Precursors (2003);

iii. Commonwealth Secretariat, IMF, and UNODC Model Provisions on Money Laundering, Terrorist Financing, Preventive Measures and Proceeds of Crime (2009)

iv. UNDCP Model Mutual Assistance in Criminal Matters Bill (2000)

v. UNDCP Model Foreign Evidence Bill (2000)

vi. UNDCP Model Extradition (Amendment) Bill (2000)

vii. UN Model Treaty on Mutual Assistance in Criminal Matters (1990)

viii. Commonwealth Model Law for the Prohibition of Money Laundering & Supporting Documentation (1996)

ix. OAS - CICAD Model Regulations Concerning Laundering Offenses Connected to Illicit Drug Trafficking and other Serious Offenses

b) *Combating the Financing of Terrorism*

i. UN Model Terrorist Financing Bill (2003)

Regional instruments

i. Organization of African Unity Convention on Prevention and Combating of Terrorism (1999)

ii. African Model Anti-Terrorist Law (2011)

iii. Eastern and Southern Africa Anti-Money Laundering Group (ESAAMLG)[151]

---

[151] The Eastern and Southern Africa Anti-Money Laundering Group (ESAAMLG) is a Regional Body subscribing to global standards to combat money laundering and financing of terrorism and proliferation. Its 18 Member Countries are Angola, Botswana, Eswatini, Ethiopia, Kenya, Lesotho, Madagascar, Malawi, Mauritius, Mozambique, Namibia, Rwanda, Seychelles, South Africa, Tanzania, Uganda, Zambia and Zimbabwe and includes a number of regional and international observers such as AUSTRAC, Commonwealth Secretariat, East African Community, FATF, IMF, SADC, United Kingdom, United States of America, UNODC, World Bank and World Customs Organization. The United Kingdom and United States of America have been cooperating and supporting nations of the organization since it was established in 1999. The main objectives of ESAAMLG are to: (a) Adopt and implement the 40 Recommendations of the FATF; (b) Apply anti-money laundering measures to all serious crime; (c) Implement measures to combat the financing of terrorism and (d) Implement any other measures contained in the multilateral agreements and initiatives relevant to prevention and control of laundering of proceeds of all serious crimes and the financing of terrorism and proliferation of weapons of mass destruction.

5.3 AML/CFT Legislation: National

Zambia has a plethora of statutes and pieces of legislation mirrored on the international models aimed at combatting ML/TF. These pieces of legislation have created a number of institutions, as will be seen below, aimed at combatting the vices both internally and externally in collaboration with other countries. The following are the laws aimed at combatting ML/TF:[152]

i.   Prohibition and Prevention of Money Laundering Act
ii.   Anti-Terrorism Act
iii. Forfeiture of Proceeds of Crime Act
iv.   Financial Intelligence Centre Act
v.   Public Interest Disclosure (Protection of Whistleblowers) Act
vi.   Mutual Legal Assistance in Criminal Matters Act
vii. Plea Negotiations and Agreements Act
viii. Anti-Corruption Act
ix.   Non-Governmental Organisations Act
x.   The Penal Code Act

5.4 Institutional Framework to Combat ML/TF

The institutional framework combatting economic crimes has been discussed at length under Chapter 2. However, at the pain of repetition, the following are institutions specifically established to counter, investigate and

---

[152] Adapted from https://www.fic.gov.zm/aml-cft-framework

prosecute ML/TF in this jurisdiction:[153]

   i.   Anti-Money Laundering Authority (AMLA)

   ii.   Task Force of Senior Officials on AML/CFT matters

   iii.   The Financial Intelligence Centre

   iv.   National Anti-Terrorism Centre

   v.   Law Enforcement Agency (LEAs)[154]

   vi.   Supervisory Authorities[155]

   vii.   Reporting Entities[156]

   viii.   National Prosecution Authority

---

[153] id

[154] Zambia Police Force; Zambia Security Intelligence Service; Immigration Department; Drug Enforcement Commission; Anti-Money Laundering Investigations Unit; Anti-Corruption Commission; Zambia Revenue Authority; and other investigative institutions that the Minister may, by statutory Instrument designate as per section 2 of the FICA.

[155] Governor of the Bank of Zambia, appointed under the Bank of Zambia Act; Registrar of Co-operatives, appointed under the Co-operatives Act, 1998; Registrar of Pensions and Insurance, appointed under the Pension Scheme Regulation Act, 1996; Commissioner under the Securities Act No. 41 of 2016; Registrar appointed under the Patents and Companies Registration Agency Act, 2010; Commissioner of Lands; Zambia Development Agency, established under the Zambia Development Agency Act, 2006; Licencing Committee, established under the Tourism and Hospitality Act, 2007; Registrar of Estate Agents appointed under the Estate Agents Act, 2001; Law Association of Zambia, established under the Law Association of Zambia Act; Zambia Institute of Chartered Accountants established under the Accountants Act, 2008; and any other authority established under any written law as a supervisory or as the Minister may prescribe as per section 2 of the FICA.

[156] Reporting entities are institutions regulated by Supervisory Authorities and are required to make a suspicious transaction reports concerning Money Laundering, Terrorist Financing and any other serious offences to the Financial Intelligence Centre and these include: Financial institutions e.g. Commercial Banks and Non-Bank Financial Institutions e.g. micro finance institutions; Designated non-financial businesses and professions (DNFBPs) such as Casinos, Real estate agents, Accountants; and Legal Practitioners among others as per section 2 of FICA.

ix.   Judiciary[157]

x.   Other relevant Government agencies[158]

5.5 Conclusion

This Chapter has discussed money laundering, terrorism financing and other related concepts. It has also tackled AML/CFT legislation and instruments at national, regional and international level. The various institutions established to actualise the objects of those instruments and legislation has also been navigated.

---

[157] Judicial authority vests in the courts and shall be exercised by the courts in accordance with this Constitution and other laws as per Article 119 (1) of the Constitution of Zambia (Amendment) Act No. 2 of 2016

[158] These include the Office of the Auditor General, Ministry of Home Affairs, Ministry of Mines, Ministry of Defence, Zambia Air Force, and Registrar of Societies among others which are very critical for the provision of intelligence and information related to ML/TF

118

CHAPTER

6

CUSTOMS RELATED OFFENCES

6.0 Introduction

This Chapter discusses primarily customs related offences. It must be noted that for any government to undertake developmental activities it must have money to fund those activities. The funding of these activities is only possible if that government is able to raise revenue. Thus, if the avenues of revenue are compromised by criminal activities through vices such as under-invoicing and smuggling among others then a country's developmental agenda is usually rendered impotent.

6.1 Under Invoicing

Section 141 of the *Customs and Excise Act, Chapter 322 of the Laws of Zambia* has provisions that creates offences relating to false invoices, false representation and forgery. Undervaluation of goods is closely related to false representation and forgery. Thus, it is an offence to undervalue goods as this makes that an invoice on which those goods are charged is under declared meaning that the treasury loses the actual revenue due as only less that will be collected.

The section highlighted in the foregoing provides that:

(1) Any person who -

(a) produces any false invoice or an invoice framed so as to deceive, or makes any false representation in regard to the nature, the quantity or the value of any goods or the country in which such goods were grown, produced, or manufactured;

(b) forges any document required under this Act or any law relating to customs or excise;

(c) under false pretences or with intent to defraud or to evade the provisions of this Act or any law relating to customs or excise or by making any false statement, affidavit, or declaration procures or attempts to procure any such document as is mentioned in paragraph (b);

(d) being required to make or render any report, statement, document, bill of entry, declaration, or return, or to supply any information demanded or asked for, or to answer any question, neglects or refuses to do so, or makes or renders any untrue or false report, statement, document, bill of entry, representation, declaration, return or answer, or conceals or makes away with any goods required to be accounted for by this Act or any law relating to customs or excise;

(e) imports or attempts to import, or assists in, or is accessory to, or connives at the importation or attempted importation of any goods illegally or without payment of the duty thereon; or

(f) deals with or assists in dealing with any goods contrary to the provisions of this Act or any law relating to customs or excise;

shall be guilty of an offence, so, however, that nothing in the provisions of this Act shall be taken to require any person who has acted as legal practitioner for any person to disclose any privileged communications made to him in that capacity.

(2) Any person who –

(a) uses or attempts to use any document which has been forged with intent to defeat the provisions of this Act or any law relating to customs or excise;

(b) otherwise than in accordance with the provisions of this Act, buys or receives or has in his possession any goods required to be accounted for by this Act or any law relating to customs or excise before they have been so accounted for; or

(c) otherwise than in accordance with the provisions of this Act, has in his possession any goods liable to forfeiture under this Act or any law relating to customs or excise;

shall be guilty of an offence, unless he produces evidence to show that he did not know –

(i) that the document was forged;

(ii) that duty on the goods had not been paid or secured or that the goods had not been accounted for in terms of this Act or any law relating to customs or excise; or

(ii) that the goods were liable to forfeiture; as the case may be.

(3) For the purpose of this section, the forgery of a document is the making of a false document, knowing it to be false, with the intention that it shall in any way be used or acted upon as genuine whether within Zambia or not, and making a false document includes making any material alteration in a genuine document, whether by addition, insertion, obliteration, erasure, removal, or otherwise.[159]

---

[159] See sections 342, 344 and 352 of the Penal Code

6.2 Smuggling

Smuggling is the offence of importing or exporting prohibited articles without paying the duties chargeable upon them.[160] It is the fraudulent taking into a country, or out of it, merchandise for which duty has not been paid, or goods the importation or exportation whereof is prohibited.[161] In the case of *Williamson v U.S.*, the word "smuggle" was construed in the following ways:

> "smuggle" has well-understood meaning at common law, signifying bringing on shore, or carrying from shore, of goods, wares, and merchandise for which duty has not been paid, or goods the importation or exportation whereof is prohibited.[162]

It must be noted that section 32 (1) of the Customs and Excise Act is instructive in that it provides that goods shall not be imported into Zambia without entry being made and without such duties as may be imposed by law being paid or secured. Similarly, section 48 (1) of the same Act provides that goods shall not be exported from Zambia without entry being made and without such duties as may be impressed by the law being paid or secured. Thus, the importation and exportation of goods without payment of

---

[160] Nolan, J.R. and Nolan-Haley, J.M. (1990). Black's Law Dictionary, 6th edn., Minnesota: West Publishing Co. at p.1389

[161] id

[162] C.A. Cal., 310 F.2d 192, 195; see also Dunbar v U.S., 156 U.S. 185, 15 S.Ct. 325, 39 L. Ed. 390

duties is criminalised.

Notwithstanding the foregoing, the law relating to smuggling in this jurisdiction is found under section 149 of the Customs and Excise Act. Related to the contents of this provision is section 140 of the same Act in as far as failing to declare goods upon arrival into this country is concerned. The two sections stated above provide as follows:

149. Any person who -

(a) smuggles or attempts to smuggle any goods; or

(b) aids, assist, or connives at the smuggling or attempted smuggling of any goods; shall be guilty of an offence.

140. Any person who, on or after arriving in Zambia, is questioned by an officer as to whether he has upon his person or in his possession any goods, whether dutiable or otherwise, or goods the importation of which is prohibited or restricted, and who denies that he has any such goods upon his person or in his possession, or fails to mention any dutiable, prohibited, or restricted goods which he has upon his person or in his possession, shall be guilty of an offence if such goods are discovered to be or, at the time of denial or of the

statement, to have been upon his person or in his possession.

6.3 Conclusion

This Chapter has briefly, yet succinctly, traversed the two most common customs related offences. These two offences have direct consequential effects on the economic outlook and stability of the country. It is important to note that all countries depend on revenue in order to sponsor all economic and social activities. It is thus a no-brainer that without this revenue no economic progress and national development can be recorded.

CHAPTER
7

FORFEITURE LAWS

7.0 Introduction

This Chapter will traverse forfeiture laws as they apply to this jurisdiction. Zambia, like many other countries, has put in place provisions that make it possible for one to forfeit proceeds of crime and finances corruptly acquired through crimes like money laundering, corruption and may others.[163] Forfeiture of property, it must be noted, is one of the penalties provided for under criminal statutes which apply to property used in the commission of a crime as well as property acquired from proceeds of the crime.

7.1 Civil forfeiture *versus* criminal forfeiture

The laws in this jurisdiction recognises the existence of both civil and criminal forfeiture. The two both result in the seizure and forfeiture of property[164] used in either the

---

[163] See sections 62 and 75 of the AC Act as an example

[164] Section 2 of the Forfeiture of Proceeds of Crime Act No. 19 of 2010 defines "property" includes any real or personal property, money, things in action or other intangible or incorporeal property, whether located in Zambia or elsewhere and includes property of corresponding value in the absence of the original illegally acquired property whose value has been determined.

commission of a crime or being proceeds of crime[165] with the only difference in the way they operate.[166] Chitengi tries to conceptualise the two concepts when he opines that:

There are two ways in which property may be forfeited, namely through the use of criminal proceedings or by using the civil procedure. Criminal forfeiture is the type of forfeiture in *personam* whereas civil forfeiture is forfeiture in *rem*. In the case of criminal forfeiture it is the person (the owner of the property) who is on trial, while in the case of civil forfeiture it is the property itself that is being tried. Therefore, the standard of proof is lower in the latter than in the former for the obvious reason that unlike a mere property, human beings bear the constitutional right to be presumed innocent until proven guilty through the rigorous process in which the prosecutor must prove his/her case

---

[165]Section 2 of the Forfeiture of Proceeds of Crime Act defines "proceeds of crime" in relation to a serious offence or a foreign serious offence, means property or benefit that is wholly or partly derived or realised directly or indirectly, by any person from the commission of a serious offence or a foreign serious offence; wholly or partly derived or realised from a disposal or other dealing with proceeds of a serious offence or a foreign serious offence; (c) wholly or partly acquired proceeds of a serious offence or a foreign serious offence;
and includes, on a proportional basis, property into which any property derived or realised directly from the serious offence or foreign serious offence is later converted, transformed or intermingled, and any income, capital or other economic gains derived or realised from the property at any time after the offence; or (d) any property that is derived or realised, directly or indirectly, by any person from any act or omission that occurred outside Zambia and would, if the act or omission had occurred in Zambia, have constituted a serious offence.

[166] Part II of the Forfeiture of Proceeds of Crime Act provides for both criminal and civil forfeiture. Division 4 of Part II, that is sections 27 to 31 of the same Act provides specifically for civil forfeiture.

against the accused person beyond reasonable doubt. In contrast, under civil forfeiture, the prosecutor simply has to allege (not prove) that there is probable cause to believe that the property about to be forfeited is involved in an illegal activity. Once he so alleges, the burden of proof shifts to the owner of that property who should prove that there is no nexus between the alleged criminal activities and the property. The onus is, thus, on the defence and not the prosecutor. This is one reason why, in practice, prosecutors opt for civil forfeiture.[167]

7.2 Possession of property suspected of being proceeds of crime

The offence

The offence of possession of property suspected of being proceeds of crime is found under section 71 of the Forfeiture of Proceeds of Crime Act of 2010. The relevant section provides that:

> (1) A person who, after the commencement of this Act, receives, possesses, conceals, disposes of or brings into Zambia any money, or other property, that may reasonably be suspected of being proceeds of crime commits an offence and is liable upon conviction to—
>
> (a) if the offender is a natural person,

---

[167] Justine Sipho Chitengi, 'Pertinent Legal Issues and Impediments Fettering the Successful Prosecution of the Crime of Money Laundering and its Predicate Offences in Zambia: Proposed Reforms,' LLM Thesis (UWC, 2009) at pp.16-17

imprisonment for a period not exceeding five years; or

(b) if the offender is a body corporate, a fine not exceeding seven hundred thousand penalty units.

(2) It is a defence under this section, if a person satisfies the court that the person had no reasonable grounds for suspecting that the property referred to in the charge was derived or realised, directly or indirectly, from any unlawful activity.

(3) The offence under subsection (1) is not predicated on proof of the commission of a serious offence or foreign serious offence.

Section 75 of the AC Act is also instructive as it provides that the provisions of the Forfeiture of Proceeds of Crime Act, 2010, shall apply in relation to the seizure and forfeiture of any proceeds or property corruptly acquired by any person and any other related matters. This provision extends the applicability of the Forfeiture of Proceeds of Crime Act to offences under the AC Act.

Burden of proof and the death of the presumption of innocence?[168]

There has been growing debate as to whether forfeiture laws are constitutional or their compatibility to human

---

[168] This part was extracted from Chapter 8 in Chirwa, J. (2020).Chirwa's Treatise on Criminal Justice Management in Zambia. Mauritius: Lambert Academic Publishing

rights. The burden of proof is a party's duty to prove a disputed assertion or charge and this includes both the burden of persuasion and the burden of production.[169] In the celebrated case of *Woolmington v Director of Public Prosecutions*[170] the House of Lords held that "throughout the web of the English criminal law one golden thread is always seen, that is the duty of the prosecution to prove the prisoner's guilt...the principle...is part of the common law of England and no attempt to whittle it down can be entertained". As Professor Kulusika also adds perspective when he notes that that:

> In general, criminal law gives the accused the benefit of doubt. The trial court may not convict an accused person unless it is shown that the accused was guilty. The prosecution must prove that the accused committed the offence charged. This must be proved beyond reasonable doubt.[171]

On the other hand, the presumption of innocence is a fundamental principle that a person may not be convicted of a crime unless the prosecution proves that person's guilt beyond any reasonable doubt, without any burden placed on that person to prove his innocence.[172] In short, an accused person is deemed innocent until proven guilty.

---

[169] Black's Law Dictionary at p. 223
[170] (1935) AC 462
[171] Simon E. Kulusika (2006). Text, Cases and Materials in Criminal Law in Zambia. Lusaka: University of Zambia Press at p.31
[172] Black's Law Dictionary at p. 1306

In *Coffin v. United States*[173] it was stated that:

> A presumption of innocence in favour of the accused is the undoubted law, axiomatic and elementary, and its enforcement lies at the foundation of the administration of our criminal law.

Thus, the common law position is that an accused person is innocent until proven guilty by the prosecution. The accused person has no burden of proving their innocence as they can also elect to remain silent. Indeed, in agreeing with this Malila, JS in reading the judgement of the Supreme Court in the case of The People v Austin Chisangu Liato[174] opined that:

> The burden of proving the guilt of an accused person lies on the prosecution who may discharge that burden beyond reasonable doubt. We agree that burden of proof in criminal proceeding lies and remains throughout on the prosecution to prove its case against the accused person beyond reasonable doubt.[175]

The Constitution of Zambia has long recognised the doctrine of presumption of innocence and the principle of burden of proof. Article 18 (2) of the Constitution provides, inter alia, that:

---

[173] 156 U.S. 432 (1895)
[174] Appeal No. 291/2014
[175] At p.J34

Every person who is charged with a criminal offence –

(a) shall be presumed to be innocent until he is proved or has pleaded guilty;

(b) ......

Despite this fact, the Constitution has provided derogations to the presumption of innocence and the burden of proof whereby in "appropriate instances" the accused may be called upon to prove his innocence thereby calling upon that accused person to provide evidence in order to prove their innocence thereby bearing the burden of proof. The Supreme Court in Zambia in the *Austin Chisangu Liato* case had this to say on this position:

> We agree that burden of proof in criminal proceeding lies and remains throughout on the prosecution to prove its case against the accused person beyond reasonable doubt. However, despite the ringing phrase of Viscount Sanky LC in the timeless case of Woolmington v. DPP regarding this 'golden thread of English criminal law', the presumption of innocence and the onus of proof which it entails, the law does, in appropriate instances, cast the evidentiary burden on the accused person to prove certain facts.

For the avoidance of doubt, we must state that the fundamental law of the land, the Constitution of Zambia, does recognize this reality. Article 18(12) of the Constitution of Zambia provides that:

"Nothing contained in or done under the authority of any law shall be held to be inconsistent with or in contravention of paragraph (a) of clause (2) to the extent that it is shown that the law in question imposes upon any person charged with a criminal offence the burden of proving particular facts."[176]

In this regard, the position of presumption of innocence and the burden of proof may be said to change depending on the law being used as the Constitution has recognised that in appropriate instances the accused may be presumed guilty until that accused person proves their innocence and hence they bear the burden of proof.[177]

Guilty until proven innocent: forfeiture laws

It can be stated from the foregoing that the burden of proof and presumption of innocence have been fiddled with is that of forfeiture laws. In driving home this proposition Soko notes that:

---

[176] At pp. J34-J35
[177] section 319 of the Penal Code, chapter 87 of the laws of Zambia is a classic example of legislation that shifts the burden on the accused person to prove certain facts

Forfeiture [laws are] heavily criticised as being a blatant violation of the right to the presumption of innocence because the proceedings are not premised on the lawful origin of the property. The parties are placed on an equal footing and the alleged perpetrator of the crime bears the burden of proving the lawful origin of the assets. If the person is unable to prove the lawful origin of the assets, this may result in forfeiture.[178]

The case of *Austin Chisangu Liato* above had opportunity to test the constitutionality of section 71 of the Forfeiture of Proceeds of Crime Act No. 19 of 2010, of the laws of Zambia. Section 71 deals with being in possession of property suspected of being proceeds of crime and all the state needs to have is a "reasonable suspicion' that the property one owns or has in possession are proceeds of crime. The onus of proving that indeed those properties are not proceeds of crime lies on the accused person hence shifting the burden of proof and reversing the presumption of innocence. The Supreme Court in the *Austin Chisangu Liato* case reasoned that:

We have carefully considered the opposing arguments of the parties on this ground. It

---

[178] Cassandra Soko, 'An Evaluation of Zambia's Asset Recovery Laws,' LLM Thesis (UWC, 2013) at p. 63

seems that the arguments are confined to interpretation of section 71 (2) of the Forfeiture of Proceeds of Crime Act, and more particularly what requires to be proved and on whom lies the burden of proof.

The learned trial Magistrate found that section 71 (2) of the Act placed the onus on the accused person to satisfy the court that he had no reasonable ground to suspect that the money had been derived from unlawful activity. That section provides that: -

"It is a defence under this section, if a person satisfies the court that the person had no reasonable grounds for suspecting that the property referred to in the charge was derived or realized, directly or indirectly from unlawful activity.

The High Court reasoned, from the stand point of the general criminal law position, that the prosecution bears the burden to prove its case against the accused beyond reasonable doubt. The court did not think that subsection 2 of section 71 of the Act suggested any reversal of the general position on who bears the burden of proof; that although the subsection did require of the accused person to plead, if he so wishes, his innocent state of mind, that is to say that he had no reasonable grounds to suspect the property to be from criminal activity, it did not shift the burden on to the accused to establish the ingredients of the offence.

Our understanding of section 71 (2) is that it does not impose any duty on the accused person to prove any ingredient of the offence under section 71 (1). Where the prosecution proves its case against the accused under section 71 (1), it behoves such accused person, if desirous of defending himself, to show that he had no reasonable grounds for suspecting that the property to which the charge under section 71 (1) related, was derived from criminal activity. While we agree with the High Court that section 71(2) does not impose any obligation on the accused person to prove any ingredient of the offence under section 71 (1), it does afford the accused an opportunity to explain the absence of reasonable grounds on his part, for suspecting that the property he was found in possession of under section 71(1) was proceeds of crime.[179]

7.3 Conclusion

This chapter has discussed the nature of forfeiture laws in this jurisdiction. It has been shown that forfeiture laws apply to any property that may have been used in the commission of a crime or that is suspected to be proceed

---

[179] At pp. J33-J34, J36

of crime. In the epilogue of the chapter, a discussion has been had to show that the forfeiture laws have shifted the burden of proof from the accuser to the accused. The laws only require the accuser to have a reasonable belief that the property in question was used in the commission of a crime or is proceed of crime and the accused is called upon to give an exculpatory explanation in the absence of which that accused may be found wanting.[180]

---

[180] See also sections 22 (possession of unexplained property) and 66 (presumption of corrupt intent) on how the burden has been moved to the accused

CHAPTER

8

TAX RELATED OFFENCES

8.0 Introduction

This Chapter seeks to discuss tax related offences generally and specifically tax evasion and tax avoidance. It must be noted that tax is a core component of a country's revenue base. It follows that if tax payers either evade or avoid taxes then a country's tax base is affected negatively and the treasury coffers run dry of cash. A tax is a charge by the government on the income of an individuals, both artificial and natural; trusts as well as the value of an estate or gift and the main objective of assessing tax is to generate revenue for the purchase and provision of public goods and services. There are many examples of taxes in this jurisdiction which may generally be grouped into income tax and expenditure tax.[181]

8.1 Tax evasion

The legal definition of tax evasion is that it is "the non-payment of taxes by means of not reporting all taxable income, or by taking unallowable deductions. It is a crime in which an individual or entity intentionally underpays, or

---

[181] See Part III of Singh, S.K. (1982). Public Finance in Theory and Practice. New Delhi: S. Chand and Company (Pvt) Limited

avoids paying taxes. It is the illegally paying less in taxes than the law permits; committing fraud in filing or paying taxes.[182] This offence involves actions such as underreporting invoices, falsifying income records and returns, wilfully underpaying taxes, inflating expenses and deductions, concealing and hiding money as well interest.[183]

8.1.1 Income Tax Act

The Income Tax Act, Chapter 323 of the Laws of Zambia is the primary legislation that governs the taxation of income in Zambia and by this Act all profit making individuals, both natural and artificial, have an obligation to pay income tax on their profits.[184]The same is true of all

---

[182] Black's Law Dictionary at p.1461

[183] Office of the Counsel General Criminal Tax Division, 'Tax Crimes Handbook,' IRS (2009) at pp.2-30

[184] www.zra.org.zm>tax-information [accessed 26/02/2021 at 17:26 PM]; section 14 of the Income Tax Act, Chapter 323 of the Laws of Zambia provides as follows: 14. (1) Subject to the provisions of this Act, tax shall be charged at the rates set out in Part III of the Charging Schedule for each charge year on the income received in that charge year (a) by every person from a source within or deemed to be within the Republic; and
(b) by every person ordinarily resident within the Republic by way of interest and dividends from a source outside the Republic.
(2) In the case of an individual, any income received as specified in subsection (1), other than income received by way of a lump sum payment and income which the Commissioner-General is prohibited from including in any assessment under the provisos to subsection (1) of section sixty-three, shall, before the charge of tax, be abated, pursuant to the Charging Schedule, by such tax credits as, under paragraphs 8A and 9 of the Charging Schedule, he is entitled to, and claims, in respect of the charge year in which the said income is received by him:
Provided that for the purposes of this subsection, "lump sum payment" excludes such payments as are referred to in paragraph (c) of the definition of "lump sum payment" contained in section two.

persons in employment who have an obligation to pay income tax on their emoluments.[185] Parts IX and X of the Income Tax Act provides for substantive offences and penalties for tax evasion in this jurisdiction as follows:

PART IX

(AVOIDANCE)

Transactions designed to avoid tax liability

95. (1) Where the Commissioner-General has reasonable grounds to believe that the main purpose or one of the main purposes for which any transaction was effected (whether before or after the commencement of this Act) was the avoidance or reduction of liability to tax for any charge year, or that the main benefit which might have been expected to accrue from the transaction within the three years immediately following the completion thereof, was the avoidance or reduction of liability to tax, he may, if he determines it to be just and reasonable,

---

(3) In the case of any individual, the charge of tax on any income referred to in subsection (2) shall be abated by the amount of a tax credit, pursuant to the Charging Schedule.

(4) The provisions of this Part, and of the First Schedule, relating to particular forms of income, are without prejudice to the generality of the charge of subsection (1).

[185] Article 266 of the Constitution defines "emoluments" to include salaries, allowances, benefits and rights from an individual's remuneration for services rendered, including pension benefits or other benefits on retirement.

direct that such adjustments shall be made as respects liability to tax as he considers appropriate to counteract the avoidance or reduction of liability to tax which would otherwise be effected by the transaction.

(2) Without prejudice to the generality of the powers conferred by subsection (1), the powers conferred thereby extend to-

(a) the charging with tax the income of persons who, but for the adjustments, would not be chargeable with any tax or would not be chargeable to the same extent;

(b) the charging of a greater amount of tax than would be chargeable but for the adjustments; and

(c) the giving of a direction under this section by reason of the fact that in the case of a company no distribution of dividends has been made or only a smaller distribution has been made than might have been made:

Provided that-

(i)   where a charge is made under this section on any company in respect of adjustments which affect the liability to tax of the income of any shareholder, such company shall be entitled to recover from such shareholder the amount of tax attributable to the adjustment made in respect of such shareholder; and

(ii) where an adjustment made under this section relates to any distributable profits of a company and such profits are subsequently distributed, appropriate adjustments shall be made in respect of the tax paid or payable by the company and the shareholders in such company.

(3) Any direction of the Commissioner-General under this section shall specify the transaction giving rise to the direction and adjustments as respects liability to tax which the Commissioner-General considers appropriate.

PART X

(OFFENCES AND PENALTIES)

General penalty

98. Any person guilty of an offence against this Act shall, unless any other penalty is specifically provided therefor, be liable on conviction therefor to a fine not exceeding ten thousand penalty units or to imprisonment for a term not exceeding twelve months, or to both.

Penalty for failure to comply with notice, etc.

99.   Every person who-

(a) without just cause shown by him fails to furnish a full and true return in accordance with the requirements of any notice served upon him under this Act or fails to give notice to the Commissioner-General as required by section forty-five or by subsection (2) of section forty-six; or

(b) without just cause shown by him fails to furnish within the required time to the Commissioner-General or to any other person any document which under this Act or under any notice served on him under this Act he is required so to furnish; or

(c) fails to keep any records, books, accounts or documents that he is required to keep under this Act; or

(d) fails to produce any document for the examination or inspection of the Commissioner-General or other person in accordance with the requirements of this Act; or

(e) without just cause shown by him fails to attend at a time and place in accordance with the requirements of any notice served on him under this Act; or

(f) without just cause shown by him fails to answer any question lawfully put to him or to supply or furnish any information lawfully required from him under this Act; or

(g) otherwise contravenes or fails to comply with any of the provisions of this Act or of any regulations made thereunder, or fails to comply with any requirements of the Commissioner-General lawfully made under this Act or under any of the Schedules thereto; or

(h) obstructs or hinders any officer acting in the discharge of his duty under this Act;

shall be guilty of an offence against this Act.

Penalty for incorrect returns, etc.

100. (1) Every person who negligently or through wilful default or fraudulently-

(a) fails to furnish a return of income in accordance with the requirements of sub-section (2) of section forty-six;

(b) makes an incorrect return by omitting therefrom or understating therein any income of which he is required by this Act to make a return;

(c) gives any incorrect information in relation to any matter affecting his own liability to tax or the liability to tax of any other person; or

(d) submits any incorrect balance sheet, account, or other document; shall pay a penalty equal to-

(i) in the case of negligence, fifty per centum of the amount;

(ii) in the case of wilful default, the amount; or

(iii) in the case of fraud, one hundred and fifty per centum of the amount; of any income omitted or understated, or any expenses overstated, in consequence of such failure, incorrect return, information or submission.

(2) Every person or partnership who fails to furnish a receipt to the payee within the time stipulated under subsection (7) of section eighty-two A shall pay a penalty equal to five per cent of the gross amount of the rent for each month or part thereof elapsing between the due date for furnishing the receipt and the date on which the receipt is furnished to the payee of the rent.

(3) The penalties provided by this section are a debt due to the Government and shall be treated as if they were tax for the purpose of recovery and shall be recoverable accordingly whether or not any proceedings are commenced for any offence against this Act arising out of the same facts.

(4) The Commissioner-General may accept a pecuniary settlement instead of taking proceedings for the recovery of a penalty under this section and may, in his discretion, mitigate or remit any penalty or stay or compound any proceedings for recovery thereof and may also after judgment in any proceedings under this Act further mitigate or entirely remit the penalty.

(5) Notwithstanding anything contained in Part XI, where in any appeal against an assessment which includes penalty, one of the grounds of appeal relates to the charge of such penalty then the decision of the Tax Appeal Court in relation to such ground of appeal shall be confined to the question as to whether or not the failure, claim, understatement or omission which gave rise to the penalty under subsection (1) was due to any neglect, wilful default or fraud.

Penalty for fraudulent returns, etc.

102. (1) Any person who wilfully with intent to evade or to assist another person to evade tax-

(a) omits from a return made under this Act any income which should under this Act be included therein; or

(b) makes any false statement or entry in any return under this Act; or

(c) gives any false answer, whether verbally or in writing, to any question or request for information asked or made in accordance with the provisions of this Act; or

(d) prepare or maintains or authorises the preparation of maintenance of any false books of account or other records, or falsifies or authorises the falsification of any books of account or records; or

(e) makes use of any fraud, art or contrivance whatsoever or authorises the use of any such fraud, art or contrivance; or

(f) makes any fraudulent claim for the refund of any tax; shall be guilty of an offence and on conviction shall be liable to a fine not exceeding thirty thousand penalty units or to imprisonment for a term not exceeding three years, or to both.

(2) Whenever in any proceedings under this section it is proved that any false statement or entry is made in any return furnished under this Act by or on behalf of any person or partnership, or in any books of account or other records maintained by or on behalf of any person or partnership, that person or the partners shall be presumed, until the contrary is proved, to have made that false statement or entry with intent to evade tax.

Bodies corporate

103. Where any offence under this Act has been committed by a body corporate, every person who, at the time of the commission of the offence was a director, general manager, secretary or other similar officer of such body corporate or who was acting or purporting to act in any such capacity, shall also be guilty of that offence, unless he proves that the offence was committed without his knowledge or consent, and that he exercised all such diligence to prevent the commission of the offence, as he ought to have exercised, having regard to the nature of his functions in such capacity and in all the circumstances.

8.1.2 Value Added Tax

The primary law relating to Value Added Tax (VAT) in Zambia is the VAT Act, Chapter 331 of the Laws of Zambia and subsidiary legislation as promulgated by the Minister responsible for finance and the Commissioner-General as found in regulations and rules. VAT is collected at each stage in the chain when value or an incremental figure (mark-up) is added to goods or services and, is applicable to all businesses in the production chain that is from manufacture to retail. VAT is also levied on imports.[186]

PART III

ACCOUNTING FOR AND PAYMENT OF TAX

Tax returns

16. (1) Every taxable supplier shall, in respect of each prescribed accounting period, lodge with the Commissioner-General a tax return, in a form approved by the Commissioner-General, containing such information as the form requires

---

[186] See Zambia Revenue Authority, 'VAT Guide,' available at www.zra.org.zm [Accessed on 26/02/2021 at 18:20 PM]; section 8 of the VAT Act provides that: 8. (1) A tax, to be known as value added tax, shall be charged, levied, collected and paid in respect of (a) every taxable supply of goods or services in Zambia, other than a zero-rated supply; and

(b) every taxable importation of goods into Zambia; that takes place on or after the tax commencement day.

(2) The reference in sub-section (1) to a supply of goods or services in Zambia includes a reference to a supply that, by the operation of section eleven or twelve or of any rule made under those sections, is to be regarded as taking place in Zambia. (3) Tax on a supply of goods and services is payable by the supplier of the goods or services and, subject to any other provision made by or under this Act in relation to accounting, is due and payable at the time of supply. (4) Tax on an importation of goods shall be charged as if it were a duty of customs under the Customs and Excise Act, and is payable, accordingly, by the importer of the goods. Section 9 of the same Act provides that: 9. (1) Tax on a taxable supply of goods or services shall be charged on their taxable value, at the prescribed rate of tax. (2) Tax on a taxable importation of goods shall be charged on their taxable value, at the prescribed rate of tax.

(3) The prescribed rate of tax shall be seventeen and a half per centum, unless the Minister, by statutory order, determines a lower rate. (4) For the purposes of any provision of this Act, or of the regulations or rules made under this Act, the prescribed rate of tax in the case of a zero-rated supply shall be regarded as zero.

in relation to the supply by him of goods or services, and the importation of goods, during that period, any tax deductions or credits and any other matter concerning his business.

(2) The return shall be lodged within twenty-one days after the end of the prescribed accounting period to which it relates or within such other time as the Commissioner-General may in a particular case determine by notice.

(3) For the purposes of this Act, the prescribed accounting period for a taxable supplier shall be the month next succeeding the month in which he was registered and each succeeding calendar month, unless the Commissioner-General, by notice in writing to a particular supplier, determines another prescribed accounting period for that supplier.

(4) A form of return approved by the Commissioner-General for the purposes of sub-section (1) shall, on request, be made available to any taxable supplier.

Late lodgement of returns

17. (1) A taxable supplier who fails to lodge a return within the time allowed by or under this Act shall pay additional tax consisting of-

(a) one thousand penalty units; or

(b) one-half of one per centum of the tax payable in respect of the prescribed accounting period covered by the return; whichever amount is the greater, for each day the return is late.

(2) Additional tax prescribed by this section is payable twenty-one days after the date on which it is incurred.

(3) The imposition or payment of additional tax prescribed by this section does not affect any liability of the supplier to pay any interest or penalty elsewhere prescribed in this Act.

PART V

REGISTRATION OF SUPPLIES

Failure to register, etc.

29.   A supplier who-

(a) being required to apply for registration under this Part, fails to do so within one month after becoming liable to apply;

(b) contravenes any term or condition of his registration; or

(c) not being a taxable supplier, holds himself out as such;

shall be guilty of an offence and shall be liable, on conviction, to a fine not exceeding ten thousand penalty units or to imprisonment for a term not exceeding twelve months, or both.

PART VIII

(MISCELLANEOUS)

Records and Accounts

42.   (1) A taxable supplier shall keep such records relating to the business carried on by him, and preserve them for a period of five years or such longer period as the Commissioner-General may, by notice in writing, require in any particular case.

(2)   A supplier who fails to keep any records required by or under this section to be kept by him, or who fails to keep them for the time so required, shall be guilty of an offence and shall be liable, on conviction, to a fine not exceeding ten thousand penalty units or to imprisonment for a term not exceeding twelve months, or both.

False returns and statements

43. Any person who, in purported compliance with any requirement under this Act, makes a return or other declaration, furnishes any

document or information or makes any statement, whether in writing or otherwise, that is false in any material particular shall be guilty of an offence and shall be liable, on conviction, to a fine not exceeding twenty thousand penalty units or to imprisonment for a term not exceeding two years, or to both.

Evasion of taxation

44. (1) Any person who is concerned in, or takes steps with a view to, fraudulent evasion of tax or fraudulent recovery of tax shall be guilty of an offence and shall be liable, on conviction, to a fine not exceeding thirty thousand penalty units or six times the amount of the tax sought to be evaded or recovered, whichever is greater, or to imprisonment for a term not exceeding three years, or to both.

(2) A person who deals in or accepts the supply or importation of any goods, or the supply of any services, having reason to believe that the proper tax has not been or will not be paid or that any deduction or credit has been or will be falsely claimed in relation thereto shall be guilty of an offence and shall be liable, on conviction, to a fine not exceeding thirty thousand penalty units or six times the amount of the tax, whichever is greater, or to imprisonment for a term not exceeding three years, or to both.

(3) Any goods which are the subject of an offence under this section shall, if the court convicts and so orders, be forfeited.

8.2 Tax avoidance

Tax avoidance is significantly different from tax evasion in that tax avoidance is the minimization of one's tax liability by taking advantage of legally available tax planning opportunities.[187] It may thus be contrasted with tax evasion which entails the reduction of tax liabilities by using illegal means.[188] Thus, tax avoidance uses *legal means* to minimize one's tax liabilities therefore legal as opposed to tax evasion which uses *illegal means* to reduce one's tax liabilities.

8.3 Conclusion

This Chapter has looked at tax related offences in this jurisdiction. We have seen that legally speaking, tax evasion is a crime that involves using illegal means to avoid tax while tax avoidance uses legal means to reduce certain tax liabilities. The Chapter has also highlighted the various provisions relating to tax evasion in this jurisdiction.

---

[187] Black's Law Dictionary at p.1460
[188] id

CHAPTER

9

ECONOMIC SABOTAGE AND SUBVERSION

9.0 Introduction

This Chapter will discuss other forms of economic crimes that a country may be subjected to by hostile elements both within and outside that country's borders. The common forms of such is economic sabotage and economic subversion.

9.1 Economic sabotage

The term "sabotage" has the following meanings as provided for under the Zambia Security Intelligence Service Act No. 14 of 1998:

i.   an act intended to cause damage or injury to-
   a. plant, machinery, or vita! installations used for the purposes of communications, transport, water, energy and electricity supply;
   b. buildings; and
   c. any other property; with a view to assisting any person, State or organisation that is hostile to the Republic or for purposes of furthering a subversive act;

ii.   withholding information or supplying information which has a bearing on the security interests of the Republic knowing that it will result or is likely to result in any government institution arriving at an erroneous decision.[189]

Thus, economic sabotage though not legally defined may constitute those actions that are directed at undermining a country's economy hence causing instability in that country by causing a rise in prices of essential commodities, food, fuel as well as interest rates on that country's external debt. The other activities maybe aimed at weakening that country's financial markets and causing the national currency to lose value and create an artificial inflation. In the final analysis, these activities disrupt the target country's economy.

9.2 Economic subversion

Subversion means any act constituting an offence against public order under the Penal Code or any other written law.[190] Subversive activities constitute those acts directed toward the undermining and overthrowing of a government, including treason, sedition and sabotage.[191] In its total meaning, subversion are actions designed to undermine the military, economic, psychological, or

---

[189] Section 2
[190] Section 2 of the Zambia Security Intelligence Service No. 43 of 1973
[191] Black's Law Dictionary at p.1430

political strength of a governing authority.[192] Activities that may be used to either sabotage or subvert a country's economy are hoarding,[193] counterfeiting,[194] money laundering, smuggling and drug trafficking[195] among others. All the offences discussed in the foregoing Chapters may be used as instruments for both economic sabotage and subversion.

9.3 Conclusion

This Chapter has briefly discussed the nature and characteristics of economic sabotage and subversion. It has shown that economic crimes may be used as ultimate tools to destabilize and a cripple a country's economy thereby forcing regime change through unconstitutional means.

---

[192] US Department of Defense, 'Dictionary of Military Terms,' Joint Education Doctrine Division (2010) at p.351

[193] Section 2 of the Control of Goods Act, Chapter 421 of the Laws of Zambia defines "hoarding" to mean the accumulation or hiding of any goods or commodities or any animals ordinarily held for commercial purposes, so as to prevent or manipulate the distribution or sale of such goods, commodities or animals to the public

[194] See sections 363 and 364of the Penal Code on counterfeiting of coins; sections 374 and 375 of the Penal Code on counterfeit stamps; and section 377 of the Penal Code on counterfeiting of trade marks.

[195] See Part III of the Narcotic Drugs and Psychotropic Substances Act

www.ingramcontent.com/pod-product-compliance
Lightning Source LLC
Chambersburg PA
CBHW060028210326
41520CB00009B/1047